Getting Here

Thoughts

Stories

Poems

Recollections

Selections from *Accent, West Michigan, The New Yorker
Magazines,* and the *Grand Rapids Press* used
with permission.

Some WOOD-TV studio photos by Michael Grass

**A portion of the proceeds from the sale of this book
will be contributed to Blue Lake Public Radio,
WBLV90.3 Lakeshore and WBLU88.9 Grand Rapids
the Broadcast Division of Blue Lake Fine Arts Camp
Twin Lake, Michigan
www.bluelake.org/radio
800-889-9258**

Published by Sitzmark Books 2015
946 Allen Springs Lane
Jenison, MI 49428

Cover design: Anne Huizenga
Printed by Gilson Graphics
Grand Rapids, MI - USA

Dedication

This collection of random, fugitive, sometimes audacious words could be dedicated to so many it would require a second volume to list them all. They would include all those who listened to or watched me in Marine City, Pontiac, New Brunswick, Detroit, Birmingham, Jackson, Grand Rapids, and Twin Lake and made me a part of their lives. I never lost sight of the fact that the light in which I was standing was a reflection of their acceptance and trust. My getting here is their doing and I am grateful beyond words.

The most important, of course, are the three people who shared the journey with me but for whom it's been a little less fun than it has been for me, if simply because a good part of the time they just saw glimpses of me as I sailed past. Show business was my life – but, in a very real way, it was our handicap.

My wife, Thelma, like most broadcast wives, saw almost as much of me on television as she did at home, but she never complained. The good things that have happened were better because of her.

Our son and daughter, Chip and Kim, suffered the confusion of growing up with two fathers – the little one, smiling from the glass box in the living room, and the life-size one, who came home and told them to clean up their rooms.

I think they've finally forgiven me.

Foreword

It took Rainier Rilke, the Bohemian-Austrian poet and novelist, more than two hundred words to describe the writing craft and its pull on the writer. I'd quote it here but it was too much trouble to copy it down from *The 25 Greatest Quotes About Writing*, found on the internet. As a hack writer, I lean more toward Mark Twain's philosophy: "Writing is easy. All you have to do is cross out the wrong words."

I've crossed out a lot of words in the seventy years since I discovered the pleasure of writing and, like a lot of real writers I've met, many of the words I crossed out were the ones I should have kept. I descend from a long line of quiet, reserved, sometimes reticent men – the type others would describe as men of few words. An incorrect assessment, to be sure. Bright and thoughtful, they all had plenty of words; they just kept most of them to themselves.

I was the breakout. From the cradle on, I had plenty to say – anytime, anywhere, on any subject, whether I knew what I was talking about or not. Very many years later, while I was holding forth on stage at a concert, the old folk music veteran, Chet Parker, waiting in the wings with my wife, was heard to mutter, "Windy feller, ain't he?" I'm pretty sure what her reply was.

Words and the many ways people use them have always fascinated me. I love the sound of the human voice, especially when employed in moderation and respectful of the words uttered. Even more, the written word is a source of mental nourishment without which I would starve. For me, the seemingly inevitable demise of printed newspapers, magazines, and books is a life-threatening reality of the modern age.

It wasn't until I was a senior in high school that I began to talk less and write more. On the following page, you'll learn about the tiny dynamo who was my English Composition teacher, who made me believe that we can all write. What I didn't learn from her, however, is that in producing a book, writing is the easy part. The one novel I wrote, *Uncommon Women*, wasn't so difficult because the characters did all the work. It had a beginning, a middle and an end, whereas the book in your hands is a collection of many different pieces, some long and some short, written at different times. Trying to get them into some semblance of order was a lot like trying to organize a marching band of chimpanzees.

The storied broadcast journalist Edward R. Murrow – my hero – once said, "I've not yet reached the point where my memories fascinate me." Well, I have, and a good part of this book reveals a lot of what conspired to get me here. It also contains some of what's come down my arms and out from under my fingers when there was no one around to listen to me talk. Some of it is heartfelt, some silly, some true, some made up, all of it the result of doing something I love to do: play with words.

I hope you like it.

Buck Matthews
Summer 2015

Miss Whitford

Each year, when high schools crank out another crop of graduates, I remember clearly how I felt when I was among them. High School was not a completely pleasant experience for me, academically speaking. I did okay in some things – music and English principally – and excelled in only one. In my senior year, I was captain of my Central High School Cadet company. Overall, my prospects for success in life, unless I chose a military career, were slim at best.

But I had one teacher who thought I had more potential than did most of her colleagues. Miss Bessie Whitford, a sweet little old lady who looked like she came right out of Central Casting, was my English Composition teacher (remember when they actually taught English in schools?). Miss Whitford ran her classroom like basic training. When Bessie was in command, we sat up and we shut up. She told us on the first day that in her class we would be expected to write and write well. We would respect the language, we'd use it properly, and we would *write*. She believed that everyone has the ability to compose narratives and put them on paper, but most people lack the courage – and the encouragement – to do it.

"Write!" she said. And we wrote. The jocks, the geeks, the prom queens and cheerleaders, the uniformed cadets, the winners and the losers all wrote in Miss Whitford's class. I don't know how she could stomach having to grade all that self-indulgent drivel we produced at her insistence, but nobody failed and we all came out of her class with better communication skills.

Near the end of my senior year, she stopped me on the way out of class to tell me about a city-wide patriotic essay competition to be staged by one of Washington, DC's bastions of historical tradition, the National Society of Colonial Daughters. She wanted me to enter. It wasn't a suggestion. I would write an essay and have it on her desk the following Monday, have a nice weekend. I thought it was pointless, but I wasn't about to tempt fate. I followed orders.

What *was* pointless was my disbelief in myself. The gold medal I won for that essay still hangs over my desk, reminding me every day that the real reward was Miss Whitford's belief in *me*. Today, every word I write or speak publicly is repayment for her encouragement. My greatest wish for every high school graduate is that there was a Bessie Whitford for them, too.

Discretion Advised

This page, you should be warned, is about sex. I just wanted you to know before you get all offended and start ripping the book apart and feeding it to your dog.

When my mother (calm down) was in her 91st year and a resident in the Wilson Health Care Center at Asbury Methodist Village in Gaithersburg, Maryland, she was rarely without visitors. Having worked as a clerk for many years at the Veterans Administration, then as the paid wedding and banquet coordinator for Washington's temple of Methodism, Foundry Church, and finally as manager of the Urban League's luncheon program for the homeless at the church, she had a fan club, let me tell you.

One Sunday afternoon when my wife and I were there visiting, we had to share her with her church circle, a gathering of a dozen or so elderly ladies who met regularly to study scripture, do good works, and, I wouldn't be surprised, plot the violent overthrow of the government. Many of them knew me from childhood, since my sister and I had grown up in Foundry Church, and were pretty well-informed of where we were and what we were up to. Mom had made sure they all understood I was a television star in the Midwest and - my word! - was writing a novel!

It didn't take long for that fact to become the focus of the conversation that afternoon and the old dears were full of probing questions about plot, characters, setting, expected publication date, and the like. One among them, I believe the eldest, finally released the elephant in the room and asked, "So tell me, young man, does this book have any sex in it?"

Well, up to that point, it didn't and I said so. What she said next just about cleared the room. "Well, take it from me, if it doesn't have any sex in it, nobody's gonna buy it."

I thought about that when I got back to Michigan and decided maybe she was right and what would it hurt if there was a little intimacy in the life of the married couple around whom the story was built? A few months later, when we were back in Maryland for my mother's memorial service, this same lady came up to me and asked, "How's that book of yours coming?" I told her it was finished. "You put any sex in it?" She was delighted to learn that I had. I'm only sorry that she could not be among the readers of that novel, *Uncommon Women*, which is now available for Kindle readers on Amazon.

With that in mind and hope for the success of this book, I thought it wise to follow her advice, so somewhere deep in this book, there's just a little......er......sex.

Maybe you won't notice it.

Getting Here

Though my father, whose influence I've never forgotten, died before my 15th birthday, my mother and sister lived long enough to see that I was gainfully employed and mostly not an embarrassment to the family. They could not see how it would turn out, unless their heavenly eyes are still on me - and I could do with fewer people looking over my shoulder.

The life I've been privileged to live has been eventful, colorful, exciting, sometimes scary, and frequently of more interest to others than to me - a price one pays for being a "public figure." I can't deny that it's fun to be the center of attention, something that wouldn't surprise my mother, who received my teachers' phone calls. Hometown celebrity can be all it's cracked up to be. It's heartwarming to have strangers care – even if they don't remember why they remember me.

Every kid whose family balances love with responsibility grows up believing his sky has no limits; that fame and fortune await. Heck, I knew by the time I was ten years old that I would succeed Gene Autry as America's most beloved singing cowboy. All I needed was the horse and the guitar and a place to keep the horse. When it was clear that getting the horse on the elevator to our apartment might not work, I considered other options. A few years later, as a senior in high school, a cadet officer, a record hop DJ, and graduating class Poet, my choices had broadened to possible careers in the military, show business, and writing. I tried all three.

Two painfully commonplace years at Ohio Wesleyan after

Breaking in at WSDC

five years in high school (I was bored, not stupid), coupled with a new war in Korea, made an Air Force career look good. I went in prepared to stick it out for the prescribed 20, but four years turned out to be enough. I was proud to have served, but a part time job in radio had awakened my show business chops.

I'd been told by a Washington announcer that I had a "radio voice," so I'd long thought about it. An audition at Detroit's WJR while still in the Air Force and working part time at small stations near the base, sealed the deal. They told me to keep in touch. When I left the service, I enrolled in a broadcasting degree program at Columbia University, where the courses were taught at 30 Rock by NBC staff personnel. One of the more significant events of my career occurred there one night outside famed Studio 8H, where Eddie Fisher was taping his Chesterfield Cigarettes show. Debbie Reynolds, his then wife, was in the hallway talking with some fans and just as I walked by, she stepped backward and drove a spiked heel into my left foot. I endured the pain without complaining for weeks. The memory of her apology warms me still.

Fascinating as all that was, I just wanted to get to work, so I bailed out of Columbia and went full time at the station in New Brunswick, NJ, where I'd been working weekends. Though I was doing the morning wake up show, I was staying up late, listening to the popular WJR nighttime announcer, fantasizing about what it would be like to have a job like that. Then suddenly one night he was gone, left to take a daytime job. When, a few days later, a phone call came from Detroit, asking me to replace him on WJR's all-night radio show, I knew that dreams really can come true.

In the 1950s, there were very few commercial radio stations that were the equal of "The Great Voice of the Great Lakes." With the enormous reach of its 50,000-watt clear channel signal, and its veteran on-air staff (including a full orchestra and chorus), it was simply in a class by itself. I was very fortunate to land a job at such a place after only three years in the business and I worked hard to earn it. Within a short time, my five-hour nightly "Show Without a Name," which featured a broad mix of music that didn't include rock and roll, had a loyal audience across the country and became a stopping-off point for many well-known people in show business. I began to imagine that my success would carry me back to New York and maybe a network job. And then one night, not long after the station had placed a full-page ad in the *New Yorker Magazine* promoting the show, I blew it.

For about two weeks, my show, which normally ran from midnight to 5:00 AM, was abbreviated to one hour to allow for transmitter maintenance.

On the fateful night, the engineers quit early and gave me the option to stay on if I wanted to. Though I really wanted to get back to doing the full show, I only had enough records in the studio for one hour and the record library was locked up. So, without calling someone in management – a cardinal sin - I signed off at 1:00 AM, then stayed the rest of the night to answer mail. When the Program Director came in to work, I confessed to him what I'd done.

My desk was empty before the sun went down.

Dick Osgood's story in the Free Press carried the headline, "Buck Matthews and WJR agree to disagree." Only there wasn't any disagreement to it. They were right and I was wrong and I didn't argue the point, but it hurt mightily to be forever known as the lunatic who shut down one of America's premier broadcasting operations. Dark days indeed.

There's a lovely little irony worth inserting here. Many years later, after I'd retired, I discovered that my tenure at WJR, brief though it was, apparently inspired a few young guys who would eventually have successful careers of their own. This is mentioned in four books on the history of radio broadcasting (*Voices in the Purple Haze* by Michael Keith, *Rebels on the Air* by Jesse Walker, *Rockin' Down the Dial* by David Carson, and *The Concise Encyclopedia of American Radio* by Christopher Sterling). You just never know.

The Dream Job

For a few months following my departure from WJR, a new FM station in suburban Detroit, WHFI, revived my show and gave me carte blanche (but little money) to do anything I wanted on the air. But it just wasn't the same without the big coast-to-coast audience, so I left.

Then along came television. A new station was being developed in Jackson and I was invited to assume the duties of Chief Announcer, which, to my dismay, included doing the nightly weather reports. Even though they knew I didn't know anything about weather, credibility wasn't the criteria. Filling five minutes in the 11 o'clock news was, so I developed a sort of silly, we're-all-in-this-together approach to meteorology. We invented something called "Weather in the Weather," doing the broadcasts from the sidewalk in front of the hotel where the station was located. Clumsy as it was, it caught on, eventually attracting the attention of WOOD-TV in Grand Rapids. When their weather guy left, they brought me and my nonsense in.

It might be one of broadcasting's great anomalies that for more than twenty years, one of Michigan's most successful TV stations had a clueless weather reporter. To their credit, we never pretended I was anything more than comic relief, though I did earn my stripes for sticking with it during periods of severe weather.

Looking back over the years, it's easy to see how often lemons turned into lemonade for me. Had it not been for my wacky hit-and-miss career, I wouldn't have come to Grand Rapids and gotten to do something I'd always wanted to do. After much negotiating, the station permitted me to develop a half-hour morning variety/talk show that became the highlight of my broadcast career. For nine wonderful years and nearly 2,000 broadcasts, our show provided a stage for local talent, discussed important community issues, and hosted some of the world's most fascinating people. It even earned national recognition, but good as the experts thought it was, the station didn't really see it as an asset and never gave us the budget to make it better. When the audience began to lose interest and the ratings fell, the logical move was to scrub the show. The station's new owners and management had already made the wise decision to replace me on the weather with a real meteorologist. That left them with a lame duck personality who needed something to do. So, they named me Community Relations Director and gave me a half-hour on Sundays to satisfy their community service obligations. Then I lost that job, too.

I'd been advised earlier that it was likely the new owners would be cleaning house, so it came as no surprise on the day I was leaving for vacation in 1983 when the new station manager called me into his office and with a warm handshake said, "Why don't you just not come back." I wasn't alone. Nine of my colleagues went with me. Like a vast number of other guys at the time, I was out of a job at age 54 – too young to retire, too old to start over.

This time I was rescued by Public Radio. My wife and I had been serving on the board of directors of Blue Lake Fine Arts Camp. The year before I left television, they'd put a fine arts radio station on the air. In 1985, I became Program Director for WBLV-FM and when the station's General Manager retired in 1987, I replaced him. Of course, as with the weather, I knew nothing about management. What saved me was an administration that gave me room to fail and the opportunity to succeed, and a talented, dedicated staff. I knew they were with me on my sixtieth birthday when they brought in a cake with sixty candles on it and the smoke alarm went off. Blue Lake Public Radio was the most challenging and rewarding job I ever had. For the last ten years of my career, I worked for an organization whose mission was service to the community, not making money.

And writing? Well, thanks to the Washington, DC, educational system, which taught me that we all have a voice and the right to express it, I learned to write early and just never stopped. Along the way, I've written a lot of magazine pieces and learned to tell stories reasonably well. When I retired from Blue Lake Public Radio, I wrote a novel, *Uncommon Women*. Later, I wrote *Soil, Soul, and Simplicity*, an irreverent history of the village of Marne, Michigan, and its Methodist church, my spiritual home for nearly thirty years. And now this collection of stuff that's been on my mind for a long time.

So that's how I got here. There's nothing in my life that I regret. I married above myself, have two children I'm proud of, and made a living at something that was, overall, more fun than work. There's not a lot of heavy lifting in the broadcasting field, but there's also no assurance that your job will be there when you come in tomorrow. I'm grateful to the Washington announcer who took the time to tell me I might be right for radio and glad I paid attention. For all the flat tires and U-turns I've experienced, I've still been very lucky. I've known some very good people with more talent than mine who never got the breaks and fell away. I've known others who started farther back and got farther ahead, but I doubt they enjoyed it any more than I have.

I wonder what's next.

(Poems written after River City's historic
Yellow Schoolhouse was destroyed by fire)

The Lost

Getting by on promise broken,
Spending half their lives in pain,
Dreaming dreams of love unspoken
(Or, if spoken, all profane),

Hearing angel voices shrieking
In their alcoholic fright,
Whiskied, whiskered nomads seeking
Neon campfires in the night.

The Loss

Neither red nor little ,
Mother of a displaced people,
Whitewashed walls around the seekers
And the celebrants of a growing city,
A bookmark in the pages of time,
Stone feet firmly in the riverbank,
A hundred years of keeping on
Through flood and fire –
Until yesterday.

Yesterday –
Some valueless miscreant,
Some – thing – for fun or profit,
Struck a light that blinded history.

Being Here

One of the disadvantages of living many places, they say, is that it's hard to know where home really is. Having been born in Washington, DC, raised in Maryland, and lived for short times in Massachusetts, Ohio, Pennsylvania, South Korea, Michigan, New York, New Jersey, and Michigan again, that could have been true of me. But I adhere to the motto on the Matthews family coat of arms – "Omne Solum Viro Patria Est," which translates roughly to "Every land is a living man's country" – which I interpret to mean that there's no place you can't feel at home if you want to.

Some of those places weren't exactly homey – crashing one summer at a fraternity brother's home in Pennsylvania, spending a year in a tent in Korea, sharing a tiny apartment in New Jersey with a guy who lived like a pig. But even in those places I was able to make myself at home; to feel that I was meant to be there and that things would get better. And though Maryland was once my home state, I am truly at home in Michigan, and not only because I've lived here for more than sixty years.

There is something about this wonderful place that sets it apart from all the other places where I've lived or visited. Maybe it's the proximity of the lakes. There seems to be no place in Michigan where you're very far from a creek or a river or a pond or a lake. Forests are abundant in other states, but Michigan is bearded with them. From small woodlots to National forests, we're everywhere within a short hike of the whisper of the trees and the hush that prevails beneath them. Montana has Big Skies, they say. Michigan's skies are almost electrically blue on some days and the sunsets fairly set the air afire. And there are the morning mists that make it worth getting out of bed to witness.

We have friends who feel it necessary to go south or west to warmer places in the winter and I feel sorry for them. While escaping the cold, they're denying themselves the alabaster silence of the snow pack and they miss the rolling shaded landscape within the woods that can't be seen at any other time.

And having lived in all those other places, there's something I know that Michiganders who've never left can't know. The people here are different. Spend a month in New York City and you can see how different it's possible to be when you haven't the advantage of living here. There are unpleasant folks here, too, but they're hard to find in the midst of Michigan's native niceness.

Circumstances brought me here but no circumstances could lure me away. I am, quite happily and emphatically, home.

Answers

There are three questions I've been asked frequently throughout my time in television. The reason for the first is obvious. "Did you order this weather?" was asked so often – and always in a friendly manner - that I ran out of clever ways to respond. One rainy Saturday morning at a crowded farm auction (I love them), I counted the number of times that question was asked. When it reached 25 or so, I went into the nearby town and bought a poncho that covered my head and made me unrecognizable. I felt a little guilty for denying folks the chance to poke me in the ribs, but it was getting in the way of my shopping.

I actually started hearing the second question when I first got into radio. People seemed always to be curious about my nickname. How did I come to be called "Buck?" I was born Charles Oakson Matthews, Jr., but my family always called me "Buddy," which became "Bud" as I aged into my teens. My peripheral family, however – aunts, uncles, cousins - called me "Bucky," which eventually became "Buck." That's the one that stuck, although my mother always called me "Buddy."

The third question, asked of me still, is "Do you miss television?" Well, I'd be a bald-faced liar if I said I don't miss the attention. I certainly don't miss the 17-hour work days or the long periods of monitoring nasty weather, but I do sincerely miss many of my colleagues (some of whom I still see at our twice-monthly lunches), and the challenges of producing the morning show. As I watch the events of the day unfold, I often wish I still had the forum those daily half-hours gave me to explore the needs of the community. And I miss having the opportunity to showcase the generations of talented young people who've passed by in the years since we folded our little minstrel show. One of the scrapbooks I've kept of my broadcast career is entitled "…..Better Than Working." And so it was.

Setting the Record Straight

It is not a compliment in show business to observe that someone spends too much time reading his press clippings. "Basking in his former glory," is another way of putting it. I've been guilty of saying it myself at times – before I realized that the time comes when reading your clippings is a way of remembering that once upon a time somebody thought you were interesting enough to write about. I happily confess that now and then I do that – and once in awhile, it startles me.

Case in point: A lengthy piece I just rediscovered that appeared in 1967 (oh, yes, I saved them all) following the tornado that wiped out our garage and nearly destroyed our prize 1931 Chevy. In commenting on my obvious skills as a weather reporter, the columnist wrote, "Mr. Matthews is thoroughly acquainted with his subject matter. He does not point aimlessly or uncertainly at the weather map and spout dull data from the teleprompter,"..........and so forth. (*Really?*)

Further, the writer wrote, "The greatest trait which he displays.....is his magnificent aplomb and self-possession which never fail him on the air." (*I love this stuff!*) "He was superbly controlled during last Friday's tornado.......Even when his own home was struck by the storm, he did not falter." (*He did, however, wet his pants.*) And here's the kicker: "His performance at that time must rank as one of the truly great moments in live television." (*Please, take your seats.*)

High-tech weatherman

That I was humbled when I read it nearly fifty years ago goes without saying. Reading it now, only makes me feel like a fraud. It's time to confess. During the more than twenty years that I masqueraded as a television weather reporter, I doubt there were many in the audience who were so taken in as the kind and generous reporter who praised me so highly. The truth is that as a TV weatherman, I was about as well-informed as your Aunt Maude. But I showed up on time and to my credit (*a little applause here*), I never pretended I was anything but an observer. I had no degree in meteorology. In fact, I had no degree in anything. Blame the people who hired me for putting someone on the air who was so ignorant of his specialty. Unlike those who bear the gold seal of the American Meteorological Association, I get wet when it rains.

Among the many who knew the truth, there was a smug uh-huh every time the forecast I gave on the air was wrong. This was a corporate failure to remember that *because* I didn't know diddly about the weather, all of the information I delivered was provided by the National Weather Service – and even they, armed with all the science at their command, sometimes got it terribly wrong. But there was old Buck out there on the firing line, taking the heat for the professionals. And our competitors certainly had a line on how to use my ignorance to their advantage. Before WOOD-TV wised up, WZZM-TV, which had a stable of real weather guys, started bragging on the air that "three meteorologists are better than none." I was the none they were talking about.

Weather in the Weather at WILX-TV

And if I appeared to be calm and reassuring during that awful night when a tornado blew through town and leveled my garage while my wife and children huddled in the basement and our dog blew away, it was only because I always get sleepy in the face of danger. There was a lot of eye-winking over that one, even though I was at my post, delivering the bad news. The term "poetic justice" was heard rather more often than I thought necessary. My family survived and our dog came back with a new hair-do and the well-insured '31 Chevy went on to win trophies.

Looking back, I suppose I could have earned those accolades if I'd shared with the audience the advice I'd gotten a year before from a local sage who knew a thing or two about a thing or two. He wrote that his family employed an old country formula to avoid severe weather. It only required a long wooden table and a dish pan. The plan of action was to pull the table into the front yard, remove all your clothes, get up on the table, and put your foot in the dish pan.

Scoff if you like but he swore that in three hundred years, no member of his family had been injured in a tornado while doing that.

That's the stuff you can't make up.

Riddance

(For a Recently Divorced Friend)

Stains upon the tablecloth
From gravy, soup, and beer
No longer seem so commonplace
Without His Lordship here.

The furniture is tidy,
The paper's off the floor,
No football games or baseball
On the TV anymore.

It's a better place to live in
Now that Master's gone away -
There's lesser cause for panic
In my life from day to day.

No screaming from the bathroom
When the toothpaste isn't there;
No grumbling in the dark for socks
That vanish in thin air.

It wasn't easy at the start -
His Majesty was missed.
I couldn't find the fusebox,
And I needed to be kissed.

But his going helped me learn I'm not
A child without a Dad.
I'm a full-grown individual and
For years I've just been had.

I've catered to the slightest needs
And wishes of His Grace
And never had the nerve – or sense –
To tell him to his face.

My life's a little lonelier
With Kingfish gone away.
And now and then I think I wish
He hadn't gone to stay.

And sometimes in the night I cry
And wonder what I'll do,
I really shouldn't miss him
But at times I guess it's true.

Now, time is helping me adjust
To going it alone,
And I no longer listen for
The ringing of the phone.

The children have stopped asking me
Where Daddy is today.
They somehow seem to understand
It's going to be this way.

My kids and I are coping with
A new found confidence.
We're happy and we're loving and
We don't miss the suspense

Of never knowing when or how
Our Leader would arrive.
We rarely even wonder if
He'll manage to survive.

The King is in his counting house
Now, adding up the score.
He'd likely smile a good deal less
If he knew we like it more.

Twister

As a non-meteorologist, my role as weather reporter for WOOD-TV, Channel 8, in Grand Rapids was just that. Weather happened, I reported it. Part of my job, of course, was to broadcast forecasts supplied to us by the National Weather Service via teletype. Fred Baughman and his successor as Meteorologist in Charge at the National Weather Service office, Jack Cooley, were my reliable sources and unintended mentors.

I remember coming home from church on Palm Sunday, April 11, 1965 and changing into casual clothes for an afternoon of grubbing around in my workshop. Not long after that, the phone rang, calling me back to the station because of a forecast of possible severe weather. This was not an infrequent event in the summertime and, as usual, I spent a good part of the afternoon ripping paper off the teletype and occasionally passing on whatever information we received that was pertinent to the people in our very large viewing area.

By the time severe weather actually began to impact greater Grand Rapids, I was on the air almost continually, reporting on what I was learning from the weather service pros and our reporters in the field. I had no idea of the true nature of the storm until I saw news film that night and went to the site with a film crew the next day.

There's a car in there somewhere

It was, for me, a sort of time warp because I'd seen it before. Following the Flint tornado of 1953, I was part of an Air Force communications team sent in to help restore contact with the outside world. The devastation and loss of life were greater there, but no more disrupting.

On the Monday following the Palm Sunday storm, I spent several hours on site interviewing survivors and witnesses. One of them was a young man who said he was driving on Alpine Church Road when his car was picked up and thrown over a power pole into a field. Though the story was hard to believe, there was gray paint on the door of his car from hitting a transformer at the top of the pole – and paint from his car was found on the transformer. His only injury was a scratch on his forehead.

That same day, I took a photo of a piece of 2X4 that had been driven into an interior wall of the Swan Inn, just a few inches below a wall lamp – without breaking the bulb. I had taken a similar photo in Flint, where I discovered a shovel driven into a tree up to its handle.

Familiar as we middle Americans are with tornadoes and the havoc they can visit upon the areas where they occur, we are still shocked and amazed at their enormous, unstoppable force and the tragic consequences of their passing. Just two years after the Palm Sunday tragedy, another tornado swept through the southeast part of town and obliterated my garage.

There's a legitimate question of whether tornadoes are increasing in number. For a long time, we said that there weren't more of them, there were just more people around to report them. I don't buy that answer anymore. I believe that the changes we've wrought in the global environment are, in fact, causing more severe weather. We simply have to accept the fact that the Earth, like too many of the people living on it, is no longer a benign and friendly planet.

Vox Populi
The People Speak

Early in my radio days, while doing the all-night trick at Detroit's WJR, I received a scathing letter of disapproval from someone who clearly wished I wasn't on the air. It was signed "Ex Listener." I felt it deserved a response (I always answered my mail), but there was no return address. So I went to one of my colleagues, veteran radio entertainer Bud Guest (his father was the beloved poet, Edgar A.) and asked how he dealt with that sort of thing. His response stayed with me throughout my career.

"First of all," he said, "Ex-Listener is still listening. He's just waiting for the night when they yank you off the air. Answering him would do no good. I use the ten/eighty/ten rule. The top ten percent of your audience thinks you're God. The bottom ten percent hates your guts. The eighty percent in the middle don't care one way or the other. Concentrate on those people."

So, even though I was named "National Radio Personality of the Year" in 1957 (by a small town newspaper in southern Ohio), before I got into television, my mail has never failed to keep me in my place. Here are a few examples from my years as a television weather reporter:

"The population of Lake Odessa is 1,806. I talked to all 1,806 people and I think if you ever had a friend living there, he must have moved to Woodbury."

"You come through the tube like a real phony. No one really cares what you do or think. It's a mystery why anyone would want you to speak to their group. You must do it for free."

"When we tune in for the weather report we expect some degree of common sense. Silliness is never a worthy substitute for genuine comedy."

"You are the only person on TV that turns his back to the camera, points with his hands, then puts them in his pockets. It is very plain to see that you were the only child in the family and are a spoiled brat!"

"All of South Haven has been wondering if your mind is slipping."

"You poor ignorant son of a bitch............" Well you get the idea.

A few other delights came in as a result of my deciding to dump the slicked down, BrylCream look, and adopt a little more contemporary hair style:

"Do you have a little Buster Brown suit to go with your Buster Brown haircut?"

"I love you Buck, I have for years, But your new hairdo, Has me in tears."

"Your face shows too many years for such a youthful do."

"Instead of having your locks teased and fluffed, you might better have invested your money in having your nose fixed."

Although Bud Guest's wise words helped to insulate me somewhat from the more vitriolic comments, I actually enjoyed the "hate" mail and never took it seriously. Maybe I should have, but I was pretty sure those things were written by folks who'd just had a bad day and didn't have anyone else to take it out on.

Here and there in this book are some other, more friendly and creative bits from the audience.

Equality

Lives that are parallel are rarely equal. In my case, the inequality is significant when measured against the lives of two other men I know. At one time, the three of us were pretty much lined up at the starting line, our shoes tied, our feet in the blocks, waiting for the starter's pistol. I must not have heard it go off.

When I arrived in Grand Rapids in 1961, I had about twenty bucks in my pocket. I was the newly-hired weather announcer for WOOD-TV with two years' experience and no idea what I was talking about.

One of those other guys came to town at about the same time, also with about twenty bucks to his name, and went to work for a local lumber wholesaler.

A few years later, I became producer and host of a daily morning talk and variety show on the same television station.

That same year, a staff announcer at a station in Akron, Ohio, went on the air with a similar program. In 1972, by chance, my show was recognized as the best of its kind in the nation by an organization of national TV executives.

With Phil Donahue in Chicago

The lumber guy rose to be president of the company he worked for and eventually bought out the owner. Not too many years after that, President Gerald Ford appointed him Ambassador to Italy. His name was Peter Secchia.

The Akron TV announcer's show moved to Chicago and became a network and syndication phenomenon, winning several Emmys. He married actress Marlo Thomas and retired a very wealthy man. His name was Phil Donahue.

Would it surprise you to know that I think I was luckier than either of those guys?

After all, I didn't have to live in Chicago or Italy.

The B.M.S.
Show Biz on the Grand

No kid is just a kid. Each of them is something else on its way to happen, marking time until the genes are all in place and the body and mind say, "Get on with it." And in the stage just before they hear that call, almost every one of them imagines a career in show business. They're all budding drummers, rappers, singers, dancers, talk show hosts. Okay, maybe not that last one. You can learn the others; the last one is just accidental.

Elsewhere in this book is ample evidence that underlying all the other possibilities that lay before me, some form of show business was what I secretly hoped for. Possibilities, yes. All things are possible and all that. Prospects, not so much. A shy show-off from a poor but happy family, I wasn't destined to emulate Marilyn Monroe's Schwab's Drugstore moment of discovery. I hadn't suffered, had no role model, didn't have a broken heart or an affliction to overcome – none of the rich soil of creativity so necessary to becoming an entertainer.

I bailed out of college early, did a hitch in the Air Force, got some part time radio jobs, tried college again, gave up and just went to work full time at a little radio station in New Jersey. I never got over the feeling, however, that someday my name would be up in lights. Getting into television got me a little closer, though being a weather reporter wasn't exactly the Great White Way. But when I finally persuaded WOOD-TV to give me a daytime half-hour in which to develop a variety/talk show – and to pay me a widow's mite for doing it – it felt like my time had arrived. I remember Program Director Marv Chauvin's sage advice: "Every show that goes on the air eventually goes off the air. Don't spend the money."

Like most everything else I've done, I had no plan for developing the show, no budget, and no staff. Ben Shapiro, who directed it for the first couple of years, did the best he could to dress the studio from the station's limited collection of furniture and props while I started calling up people in the arts and community organizations and, in so many words, using the old Mickey Rooney line, "My father owns a barn – Let's put on a show!" Ben picked the show's original name – "With Buck Matthews." I didn't care if we called it "How's Your Grandmother?" We were going to do a *show*!

Once the word got out that there was a window they could shout through, people started calling me. Within a short time, we were booked up to four months ahead, packing the half-hour with eight to fifteen-minute segments on every conceivable community issue, showcasing local talent, and chatting it up with celebrities who were in town for appearances. All of this while still doing my morning and evening bits in the news/weather/ sports strips and making two or three personal appearances a week. I was strung as tight as a banjo string and falling behind. I needed help and couldn't get it. I begged the station to hire someone to assist me with the bookings but no go.

Then one morning, I did a segment on City High School, an alternative program of the Grand Rapids Public School system for gifted and highly-motivated kids. It's a unique setup in which the students take their academic studies in the mornings and spend the afternoons interning with companies in their fields of interest. The guests were two students, a boy and a girl, and one of their teachers. Following the program, the teacher told me that the young lady had an interest in broadcasting and wondered if the station might have something she could do to learn more about it. I came very close to kissing her on the lips (the teacher, that is) and thus was my problem solved. Susan Braccio, a bright, mature, beautiful young woman, became my volunteer Production Assistant and her contribution to the success of the show was immeasurable. By the time she graduated, she'd made such an impression on the station that they hired her - and promptly took her away from me.

This time, my protests had traction and Suzy took on more responsibility, handling calls, keeping the booking sheets up to date, greeting guests and making them feel comfortable before going into the studio, and assisting Mike Meyer, who had become the Director in the third

Cartoonist unknown

year. By that time, it had become "The Buck Matthews Show" and was living up to all my hopes for it.

There were nearly 2,000 originations of the Buck Matthews Show over a period of nine years and I look back on it with no less than

Mike Curb Congregation

awe. It wasn't Broadway; it was better than that. It was show business on a hometown scale. It was also a town crier, a stage, and a bully pulpit for causes that didn't get enough attention otherwise. We were excited when the celebrities came to visit, of course, but equally glad to have regular local guests whose repeat appearances dealt with such topics as child raising, mental and physical health, consumer affairs, marriage counseling, book reviews, cooking and housekeeping and many others. We made mistakes now and then, but did no harm. I was criticized sometimes for my choices of guests or subjects, but invariably forgiven by the larger audience, who understood that my intent was honorable.

Of course, the guests made the show what it was – a billboard for all the good things that make Grand Rapids the exceptional place it is. And although it was a traditional studio production, we also used it as a vehicle to cover events and places that could only be seen on location. In the course of its run, we produced a number of documentaries and specials that were broadcast in our time slot. Sometimes, we rose above ourselves and good things happened. Our shows on rape, breast cancer, and mental health were credited with opening minds and encouraging victims to come forward. Our studio concerts featuring local artists or celebrity performers with live audiences were always a hit. A few of the local performers have said that their careers began on our show.

Of the three of us, of course, Mike had the most responsibility and worked the hardest. With no budget and a poorly-stocked prop house, he always found, borrowed, or stole just the right stuff to turn Studio A, which had all the charm of a dockside warehouse, into a professional-looking soundstage. He also had to deal with issues I wasn't even aware of, which included managing a crew of six or more technicians in the studio and control room. All I had to do was look cute.

Though I received a lot of recognition for what the show accomplished (Keys to the City of Grand Rapids from two different mayors, the Arts Council Festival Award, selection by the National Association of Television Broadcast Executives as the best locally-produced show of its kind in the nation), I never lost sight of the fact that the real work was done by those off-camera.

Because each of us experienced the show from a unique perspective, I asked Mike and Susan, who remain my life-long friends, about their memories of the BMS. They recalled some wonderful moments – serious, funny, inspiring, surprising – all part of the fabric of the television program that almost didn't happen and was, as predicted, cancelled after nine years.

Some of the things we remember.....

• The time a guest cook set her hair on fire practicing some sort of flambe' before we went on the air. The floor director saved her from incineration, she cleaned up in the lady's loo, and did the show with no hint of the near disaster of a few minutes before.

• The south-of-the-border group, Folklorico Mexicana (we think that's right), which failed to arrive in time to rehearse their lip-sync, which blew up in their faces when the record they brought with them skipped in the middle of the song. Served me right for having them perform.

The team—Suzy, me, and Mike

• The more than 100 appearances of creative crafter Carol Duvall, the "Queen Mother of the Trash Basket," who never failed to please the audience with her personality and ingenuity.

• The family singing group, twelve in all from parents to toddler, who arrived from Detroit in a beat-up old bus and knocked us out with their performances. Sadly, their name is lost.

• "Here Comes Festival," the outrageously ambitious special we did that included the New World Quartet performing on the roof of the County building and Amaryllis performing in the middle of the DeVos Hall construction site and the Fish Ladder.

• The beautifully detailed "painted" cakes by Rose Hale from Ionia, each depicting guests who appeared on the show.

• The gracious interacting of some celebrity guests with the studio audience – Maya Angelou answering questions from students from a local high school; Red Skelton sticking around after the show to schmooze with a little 4-H group dressed as clowns; and country recording star Marty Robbins doing the same with a group of students from Lincoln School. When one of them asked him to sing, he said he'd need a piano. So the crew rolled the piano in and he serenaded those special young people for almost an hour.

• The great "gotcha" we pulled when we were told that opera star Patrice Munsel, scheduled to perform that evening with the Grand Rapids Symphony, could not – would not – sing for us ("Don't even ask!"). I didn't ask, but we had the piano, low-lit, parked on a rug in the middle of the studio with the gifted Homer Jackson playing softly as the star walked in.

With country music's Marty Robbins

Miss Munsel and I sat on stools by the piano and chatted pleasantly about her stunning career and her concert that evening. I just happened to mention that my favorite recording of

Yoga with Nancy DeLie

hers was "Vilia" from "The Merry Widow." On cue, Homer started to play the introduction and, then and there, the opera singer who would not, under any circumstances, sing for us – sang for us. Her manager, standing in the wings, was not a happy guy.

• The cows and buffalo and horses and dogs and snakes and elephants that sometimes joined us in the studio. Of the many shows we did with animals, three are most memorable.

The buffalo, named "Little Joe," had been raised as a pet by a local osteopath, who bred bison on his Muskegon County farm. The doctor's wife had written a memoir titled "Why They Call Him the Buffalo Doctor." Joe, who was by then the size of a pickup truck, was not happy to be there under those studio lights and the doctor had all he could do to keep him from charging the cameramen – until the theme music started. Suddenly, Little Joe quit pawing the floor, flopped down, and went to sleep. The minute the show was over, he headed for his trailer, dragging the doctor behind him.

One day, we had an awful incident with two fifteen-year-old amateur herpetologists who'd brought their collection of venomous creatures. They handled the deadly snakes with confidence and skill, but we were all very much on edge. The most dangerous of the snakes was a reticulated python, which behaved badly and left an impression on us we were a long time getting over. Who knew that python poop was the most vile-smelling substance on earth?

Then there was the day we had a studio audience of little old ladies and one of our guests was the Shrine Circus elephant handler, who brought with him a baby elephant. A very friendly baby elephant he was, too. In eight minutes he managed to get his trunk up the skirt of every woman sitting in the front row of the audience.

• Of all the shows we did over the years featuring bands and choirs and ensembles and individual artists, there are two we'll never forget. One morning, we presented a one-hour concert featuring jazz giant Dave Brubeck and Sons with a studio audience of young college students. Dave took the time to engage in lively conversation with some of them. On another occasion, we managed to squeeze the entire Grand Rapids Symphony into the studio - close to a hundred musicians, three guests (including Phyllis Diller), three cameras, and me into a space half the size of the DeVos Hall stage. Mike's memory of that one is of trying to light it adequately, using every light in the grid, turning the studio into an oven.

• My personal wardrobe consisted of one suit and two sport jackets, which began to look a little seedy after a couple of hundred shows. So we swung a deal with Houseman's Department Store downtown. Once a month, they'd fit me with five sport jackets and lend them to me in turn for a "Buck's wardrobe by…." announcement at the end of each show. Most of them were much too loud for me but they did give me a more contemporary look.

• The many times we brought objects into the studio that must have given management reason to wonder why they let me do the show. Cars, boats, custom vans, airplanes……Oh, yes, airplanes. One of them was a "roadable plane," a small aircraft that could be easily converted to a car once on the ground. The other was a single engine Cessna that two ladies had flown into town and towed to the station behind a taxi with the wings strapped to the roof. We rolled it into the studio, put a wing back on, and I interviewed them while sitting in the cockpit.

Don't try this at home

• The show we did with a customized van called "The Love Machine" that had a round bed in it and a live, scantily clad model on board. She was sitting provocatively in the doorway when Mike called for a closeup and the cameraman accidentally hit the instant zoom button. For a brief, horrifying moment, home viewers had a full-screen view of the model's crotch.

• And the fact that we never drew a blank. It wasn't unusual to have guests cancel on us for reasons of illness or travel delays or, sometimes, simple stage fright – often on the morning they were to appear. But frequently, a few minutes after getting the cancellation, we'd hear from someone who wondered if we had an opening and was willing to get to the studio on the double. There's an old adage in broadcasting that goes, "When all else fails, describe the studio." We never had to do that and, now and then, those replacement segments would turn out to be better than what we'd originally scheduled.

Of course, we can't remember all of the crazy happenings, unusual guests, pleasant surprises, frightening events, and magic moments we experienced in producing nearly 2000 broadcasts of the Buck Matthews Show. But every day was unique in itself and I never lost the feeling that having the show was a privilege. Far too few have their dreams fulfilled. Mine was and I'm deeply grateful to everyone who made it possible.

The roadable plane

Droppings

One of the life lessons I learned early on, having grown up in a city awash in celebrity, was that nobody likes a name-dropper. In the nation's capital, it was a rule sometimes difficult to follow. The District of Columbia was a safer place to live and work in at that time, so security was often observed by ignoring it. Members of Congress and the Diplomatic Corps, famous though they were, didn't think of themselves as celebrities and weren't followed around by people with cameras and microphones – or weapons - all day. Many of them actually rode home from work on the bus or streetcar and came to church on Sundays with the rest of us. Even the President showed up once in awhile. Many of the Congressional kids went to school with us. To their parents' credit, they didn't consider themselves special, either.

You would think, therefore, that I would be immune to the lure of famous people; that Big Names would be no big deal to me. *Hah!* It is to *laugh*. Once I blew out of town and into life, I was as star-struck as the best of them. The modest lives of Government's movers and shakers might have made them ordinary to us native Washingtonians, but the bright lights of Show Business were another matter altogether. You had only to look at my collection of "personally-autographed" photos of half-a-dozen radio heroes, my pearl-handled Gene Autry cap guns, and my Little Orphan Annie Decoder Ring to know that I was a sucker for the famous.

With Red Skeleton

With Pat Boone

Is it any wonder then, that what I wound up doing for a living in the decade spanning the 70s and early `80s was like catnip? When my morning TV show went on the air, my intention was to be a sort of window through which the advocates of local causes could shout, and a stage on which the talented people of the community could perform. I'd no idea it would also serve as an effective promotional tool for people of note to tout their books and speaking engagements and concert appearances. Within a few months of going on the air, I found myself every few days sitting in the company of people I never thought I'd meet in a million years, carrying on casual conversations as if they were just in the neighborhood and dropped in for coffee.

With Maya Angelou

With Phyllis Diller

In looking back through the 40-year-old booking sheets, I counted more than 125 names that were among the glitterati of the time, some now dead, some whose flame is still visible in the firmament of popularity. I see or read about some of them occasionally and can't help but wonder... would James Garner have remembered our empathizing with each other over our bad backs? Would Burl Ives have recalled how we talked over lunch about our love for tree houses? Does Tom Brokaw remember laughing with me backstage at DeVos Hall about the impolite letter I once wrote him when he was host of the TODAY show? Did my adoration of Beverly Sills show too much as we chatted before I introduced her at a Junior League event? Is Jane Fonda aware that our discussion of her trip to Viet Nam brought my show national recognition? Did Phyllis Diller regret my turning down her invitation to play Ping Pong?

Or, am I name-dropping?

How Could I Ever Forget...

Rex Allen, Jack Anderson, Lynn Anderson, Melissa Sue Anderson, Maya Angelou, Ray Anthony,   Eddie Arnold, Vincent Bageta, Pearl Bailey, Christine Belford, Dave Berg, Father Philip Berrigan, Tony Bill, Dirk Blocker, Pat Boone, Joseph Bottoms, Bill Brashler, Dave Brubeck, Phillip Buchen, Art Buchwald, Jethro Burns, Godfrey Cambridge, Don Cherry, Shirley Chisholm, Dick Clark, Jan Clayton, Roger Coleman, Columbus Boychoir, Dick Contino, Buster Crabbe, Crash Craddock, Gretchen Cryer, Ken Curtis, Anne B. Davis, Jimmy Dean, Katherine deJersey, Dr. Julianne Densen-Gerber, Rich DeVos, Phyllis Diller, Jeane Dixon, Hugh Downs, Richard Durell, Ray Eberle, Lewis Engman, Nora Ephron, Barbara Fairchild, Jose Ferrer, Lillias Folan, Jane Fonda, Nancy Ford, Jimmie Forest, Four Coins, Four Diamonds, Four Joes, Four Lads, Four Voices, Four Winds, Connie Francis, Mike Frankovich, Crystal Gale, James Garner, Peter Gent, Euell Gibbons, Benny Goodman, Al Grey, Merv Griffin, Judith Guest, Janet Guthrie, Bill Hayes, Richard Hayman, Mary Hemingway, Eddie Heywood, Lois Hunt, Burl Ives, Eliot Janeway, Jimmy the Greek, Dean Jones, Stan Kann, Igor Kipnis, George Kirby, Kirby Stone Four, Virginia Knauer, Kreskin, Tom Landry, Sam Levinson, Fulton Lewis Jr., Hal Lindsey, Larry Linville, Fred Lowery, Betty Madigan, Ray Martin, Johnny Mathis, Colleen McCullough, Barbara McNair, Don McNeil, Marian McPartland, Hamish Menzies, Mike Curb Congregation, Miss America, Miss USA, Carlos Montoya, Buddy Morrow, Patrice Munsel, Anne Murray, Joe Namath, New Christy Minstrels, Nick Noble, Robert Novak, Glynnis O'Connor, Brian O'Doherty, Eddie Oliver, Dr. Linus Pauling, Pat Paulsen, Jan Peerce, Valerie Perrine, Diane Pike, George Plimpton, Jimmy Pritchitt, Bonnie Pruden, Dack Rambo, Jean Pierre Rampal, Jerry Reed, Bobby Riggs, Marty Robbins, Eileen Rodgers, Roy Rogers and Dale Evans, Wayne Rogers, Leonard Rose, Royal Lippizon Stallions, Gyorgy Sandor, Joe Santos, Jessica Savitch, Peter Schikele, Daniel Schorr, L. William Seidman, Red Skelton, Sally Stanford, Jerald Ter Horst, Danny Thomas, Burr Tilstrom, Jerry Vale, Jay Van Andel, Judith Viorst, Larry Wilcox, Andy Williams, Roger Williams, Earl Wilson, Kai Winding, Lumen Winter, Earl Wrightson, Florian Zabach, Nicanor Zabaleta, and Admiral Elmo Zumwalt?

For a half hour or so, we were very close.

The Fashion Plate

Gene! Over Here - It's Me!

I once had a very nice conversation with Roy Rogers and Dale Evans, who were guests on my show. Genuinely nice people they were, too. This was long years after they were bright stars in the entertainment firmament. Roy had been reduced to doing Lysol commercials, so it wasn't a big deal. Just as well, too, because by then I didn't have to fake being pleasant to them. You see, I never really liked Roy Rogers – though I willingly admit he was a sincere and talented man – because he had invaded what I considered to be sacred ground.

Before Pearl Harbor, the most popular and influential personality in the somewhat exclusive field of movie and radio cowboys was a Tioga, Texas, ranch hand-turned-railroad-telegrapher named Eugene Autry. The story of how Will Rogers heard him picking and singing for his own amusement one night in an Oklahoma freight station and inspired him to give up railroading for show business is legend. And by the time we were drawn into the Great War, Gene Autry was a superstar, riding to glory on a horse name Champion, dispensing equal doses of music and justice from a place called Melody Ranch, which was as real to me as my own home.

In all, Gene (his real friends could call him that) made 64 movies for Republic Pictures (I saw them all at least once) wrote and recorded almost 300 songs for Columbia Records, selling more than 30,000,000 copies. Perhaps more important, he gave me the only thing to look forward to on Sunday except for my mother's fried chicken, mashed potatoes, and cream gravy – his "Melody Ranch" radio program at six o'clock. When the magic hour finally arrived and that uncharacteristically elegant arrangement of "Back in the Saddle Again" began (saxophones and violins on horseback?), there was no reaching me until the last shot was fired and the last guitar chord faded into the station break, evicting me from the place I wanted to be more than anywhere else in the world.

I remember December 7, 1941, clearly – not because of the attack on Pearl Harbor so much as what Pearl Harbor did to Gene Autry, his show interrupted constantly for news bulletins from Hawaii. Very soon after that, he hung up his spurs and guitar to volunteer as a pilot in the Air Transport Command.

That's when that sneaky young rascal named Leonard Slye from Cincinnati put on cowboy clothes, got himself a horse named Trigger, and took over the singing cowboy business. In short order, he was being ballyhooed as the World's Greatest Cowboy Movie (and Radio) Star, Roy Rogers. It troubled me greatly that he wasn't off making the world safe for democracy, too. After all, he was younger than Gene and it was just wrong that he'd invaded territory that was the exclusive property of the original singing cowboy. And he wasn't even using his own name.

Well, Gene did all right for himself. Melody Ranch was intact when he came back from the war and we were all waiting for him to be back in the saddle. He amassed a fortune, bought himself a baseball team and a string of radio and television stations and became a big tycoon out west, wheeling and dealing in figures beyond anything he ever recovered from a stage coach robbery. By the time he died, a multi-millionaire, in 1998, I was in show business myself (still wishing I had a horse and a guitar and my own Melody Ranch). And, by then, I'd forgiven Leonard Slye.

The Ones That Got Away

As fortunate as we were in the number of celebrities who appeared on the Buck Matthews Show, there were three people we missed – and I mean missed. I admired all three and two of them would have come if circumstances had been right. The third wanted nothing to do with me.

Let's start with that one. And this gets complicated, so be patient. Steve Allen, the man who practically invented late night television entertainment, was one of the two broadcasters I admired most. (The other was Edward R. Murrow – but he was dead before my show went on the air). Allen was hands down the funniest man I ever saw. He was also an excellent musician, said to have written 14,000 songs. That's impossible, of course, but he was a prolific author, having written 50 books on various subjects. He wasn't a bad actor, either, playing the starring role in the movie, "The Benny Goodman Story."

When I learned that he would be making an appearance in Grand Rapids, I got right on it. I'd learned that it was a good idea to find a hook that would make our show seem worthy of a celebrity's time. An old band leader who'd been on the show a couple of times had worked with Steve Allen's showgirl mother, Belle Montrose, back in the twenties when she'd appeared with his band during its historic run at one of Detroit's major showplaces. So my hook was going to be to have this old show-biz veteran appear with Steve and reminisce. Except after I had all the pieces in place, Steve Allen's agent told me, "Mr. Allen doesn't do local television." Period.

I went through similar preparations for an appearance I'd been assured would take place. Country music star Porter Wagoner was coming to town with his sensational new vocalist, Dolly Parton. Well, you know which one of them I wanted to sit down next to. The front man for the show told me that Dolly loved to do shows like ours and he'd guarantee me an exclusive, so we wrote her name on the booking sheet for that date in ink. I still believed in the hook, so I set about learning everything I could about her. I talked with her high school principal in Sevierville, Tennessee, who told me what a good student she was and how obvious it was that she had a future in the music business. He even sent me a copy of her graduating class year book, from which we copied photos of her as a teenager (she stood out like a pheasant in a room full of hens) to use on the show.

Because their tour bus wouldn't get to town until late in the day for an evening performance, we offered to tape the show at 5:00 PM, an unusual arrangement because the studio had to be cleared in time for the six o'clock news. We were ready. Cameramen, audio engineer, switcher, tape operator, director, host, floor director at the door, Suzy ready to usher Dolly in. We waited until there was no choice but to break it down and get ready for the news. Their bus had been delayed and they got to town just in time to go onstage. The English language does not include a word sufficient to describe my disappointment.

The third omission was entirely my fault and I regret it greatly. I made it a policy not to interview politicians, because I didn't want to have to steer the show around their hidden agendas. It was easy to fend them off because when they called and wanted to get on right away, it was easy and truthful to tell them we were booked solid for the next four months. The one among them I'd have been happy to talk with was Jerry Ford, a native son of Grand Rapids and the only politician I knew who wouldn't have taken advantage of us. (Though I'm a Democrat, I'm convinced that we'd be living in a much more civilized country if he'd been elected President.) But he didn't call and I didn't call him because it would have set a precedent. It was a mistake I regretted for many more reasons than his ascension to the Presidency.

His suit was better than mine

But then a funny thing happened. One day I got a call from somebody (I wish I remembered who) asking me to come to Holiday Inn North for a photo op with somebody important. The details of this are a little fuzzy except I remember with clarity that when I arrived, I was ushered into a room where three secret service agents and a photographer were waiting. Shortly after that, the Vice President of the United States walked into the room, shook my hand, and made small talk with me while the photographer did his thing. After about ten minutes, Jerry said, "Nice to meet you," and left. Unless he was checking me out for a cabinet appointment, I have no idea what that was all about.

Not long after, he was back in town for his 54th high school reunion and I was invited to be the MC at the celebration breakfast. My souvenir of the event is the program, listing me as "Celebrity Guest," which he signed for me.

God, I loved show business.

Campaigning

Oasis came to mind.
In this basemented, gossiping desert
Of old people,
She was an oasis.

Twice around the room already,
Table by table, he'd made his way.
Answering the same questions,
Expressing the same opinions,
Shaking the brittle, bony hands,
Giving them the best of what was left.

Another "Trust in me" luncheon,
Politics faithfully proving again
Its kinship to life in a nursing home.
Where were the Junior League cocktail parties?
The college girls rallying in straw hats?
Nothing about it was fun anymore.

She looked up as he stopped
And he could no longer hear
The chatter of the old people –
Their voices dissolved
In the unspoken greeting of her smile.
Careful here. He moved on.

The snapshot image of her face
Remained, just behind his eyes.
She was superimposed
On everything he saw.
This circuit was quicker –
His skills were restored.
It could be fun after all.
The old ladies were charming,
The old men witty,
And here came her table again.

He was behind her, touching her shoulder.
She turned to greet him again.
She gave him her tiny, parchment-covered hand
And smiled his smile.
She'd met his father the same way
Fifty years before.

Junket
(Not the Dessert)

If I've learned anything in my eight-plus decades, it's that we're all basket cases sometimes. Even the most self-assured among us is ill-at-ease in some circumstances, and sometimes just plain scared out of our pants. Even those paragons of self-confidence, salesmen, must have the willies when the big buy is pending.

I bring this up because of an experience I had back in the late seventies when NBC gathered a bunch of local talk show hosts in one spot to meet and interview the stars of their upcoming fall series. One of those junkets was to Atlanta, the other to Hollywood. Hollywood was first. Hollywood! I went to *Hollywood*! Yessir, folks, I'll never forget the time I went to *Hollywood* to interview the *stars*!

Needless to say, I was geeked when the word came that I was on the list of local talent picked from stations all over the country to participate. NBC sent me a list of the actors I'd be interviewing, along with biographical information and brief synopses of the shows on which they'd be appearing. I went to the airport wearing the best clothes I owned, my study materials and clean underwear in my attache case, feeling certain that everybody on the plane could tell that I was On-My-Way-To-Hollywood-To-Interview-The-Stars. Or maybe they thought I was on my way to Toledo to apply for a job. I didn't care.

On the plane, I studied the cheat sheets until I could recite the facts in my sleep. When we landed in Los Angeles, I hailed a cab and told the driver which hotel I wanted. Because cabbies know everything, he was aware that NBC was hosting some big event at that very hotel. We weren't three minutes from the airport, when he reached over the seat and handed me a script he'd written for a TV show and asked me if I could get the network suits to look at it. I was never so flattered in my life. Not only was I in Hollywood to interview the stars, but this aspiring screenwriter thought I was an NBC executive! This had to be an omen.

I was pretty pumped up when I checked in at the hotel and headed for the elevator with my room key, my welcome packet, my attache case, and my ego. I dropped my stuff in my room and checked the packet to see what I was supposed to do first, and found that the local station personnel were invited to the hospitality suite for wine and cheese and conversation. So I got on the elevator and headed up about 200 floors. When the doors opened, it all went south.

I walked into a room crowded with beautiful women and handsome men, all looking like they were auditioning for parts on Broadway. The conversation and laughter were deafening and there wasn't a soul in the room who didn't look like someone the cabbie thought I was. I looked around for someone – anyone – who looked like me, an ordinary guy from the Midwest who'd been invited to the party by mistake. I was horrified – and terrified. The room absolutely reeked of self-confidence. Where the hell did these people come from? I was supposed to be sharing this experience with television announcers and news anchors from Keokuk and Wheeling and Boise – and I wind up in a room full of male models and Superbowl cheerleaders.

I did what any real man would do. I accepted a glass of wine from a passing hostess and walked out onto the balcony, where I stood for several minutes looking down at the street three miles below. I leaned heavily on the railing and sipped my wine and calculated how long it would take to get down there if I didn't take the elevator. I wondered briefly if I might have stumbled into the wrong hospitality room – prayed that I had. But the conversations inside were sprinkled with station call letters and I knew there was no escaping the fact that I was the wrong guy in the right place. Hollywood, for which I had felt so ready only a few short hours ago, was not going to be an experience I would brag about when I got back to Grand Rapids.

I didn't sleep well that night, dreading the morning when I would have to sit in a room on the mezzanine level and interview a parade of celebrities as they circulated among the rooms where those fancy people and I waited. There were three local announcers in each room, as well as a cameraman, an audio engineer, a producer and a bank of lights bright enough to send signals to Venus. The other two announcers, looking no less handsome and confident than they had the night before, pranced and pawed the floor like thoroughbreds waiting for the bell to ring and the gate to open. I sat in the corner trying to remember anything I could from the information we'd been provided. The setup was that we would take turns interviewing each celebrity, who would then move on to the next room and go through the same routine with three more announcers. I could imagine them answering the same dumb questions all day. It was the one time I was sorry for someone other than me.

On the first go-round, I went last, and it was the first time on the trip that I knew there was a merciful God. It was obvious from the first question asked that the other two people had probably not done more than six interviews in their careers. Suddenly there was oxygen in my lungs and sunshine in the room, because my show had already been on the air for five years and I had probably interviewed five hundred people, many of them as famous as the actors who were shuttling through. The day turned out to be a pleasure. James Garner and I talked about our bad backs. Burl Ives and I found we both liked to build treehouses and later had lunch together to continue the conversation. Dick Clark and I remembered our early days as disc jockeys. Valerie Perrine had lovely thighs and I don't remember a thing we talked about. And when the long, grueling day was over, I had eight or ten good conversations on tape to take back home and put on the air.

That night, when I went up to the hospitality suite, I found myself in a room full of ordinary people just like me, working stiffs who'd just spent a day in the mines doing what we did for a living. I took a glass of wine out on the balcony and stood there looking out across the neon landscape and wondered if Hollywood was ready for me.

The next year we did the same thing in Atlanta but all I remember of that junket was riding 75 floors in the Peachtree Plaza Hotel elevator with the lovely NBC news anchor, Jessica Savitch. It wasn't Hollywood.

As good as it gets

Selling the Groceries

Sometimes when I'm watching television, which I do far too much, I'm amazed by the changes that have taken place in advertising. Commercials these days are so over-dramatized, it's often difficult to figure out what they're selling. Early in my career, the standard thirty-second commercial consisted of a person (usually a man – sometimes me) standing in front of or holding up the product and extolling its virtues, real and imagined. We did most of them live (I did a zillion of them while I was the host of my morning television show), though we sometimes filmed them for later use. I much preferred doing them live because if we made a mistake, we just

The shoes were borrowed

plowed ahead, like real people. When they were filmed, we did them over and over until we got it right or they ran out of film and settled for what they had.

When tape and color arrived, we started getting a little cute, especially with spots that were produced by an outside agency. In their hands, perfection was expected because it was the agency's reputation that was at stake, not mine. I wanted to get it right, of course, but I didn't think it needed sterility. I remember doing a spot for Harvey Cadillac that was produced for their "Caddy Sale." They had two cars in the studio, one of which had a full golf bag sticking out of the driver's window. Dressed in knickers and cap, I was to walk toward the camera, pull a club from the bag, stop by the front bumper, and take a soft swing, all the while delivering the deathless prose written by the agency copywriter and printed on cue cards. The producer wanted me to use a specific hand gesture for emphasis and with everything else I had to remember, I kept blowing it. After 21 takes, it was only getting worse. He finally gave up and used number ten.

Another golden moment in show biz happened on an out-of-town shoot we did at a lumber yard that specialized in pre-fabricated houses. This one would be too complex for cue cards because I had to start in the kitchen, pick up an empty coffee cup, walk through the dining room into the living room, sit down in an easy chair and place the cup on a side table, talking all the while. This required memorizing the sixty-second script, which was not natural for me. I worked on that copy for two days before we hit the road, and continued to do so sitting in the back seat during the one-hour trip. By the time we got there, I had it down pat. I could have recited it backwards. While they were setting up the lights and making sure the props were where they needed to be, I walked around the parking lot, repeating the script over and over. I was ready. I positioned myself in the kitchen, my hand on the counter, and when the director said "Cue Buck," I picked up the coffee cup and forgot every word of the script.

It took four hours to record that one-minute commercial. Nobody spoke to me on the ride home.

Appearing Tonight

Many of us who make our living out there in front of God and everybody are surprisingly shy. As much of a show-off as I was growing up, there was a bit of all-talk-no-action in me as an adult. On the air, I could speak without faltering to the hidden multitudes, but standing up in front of a roomful of Kiwanians or Junior Leaguers filled me with unreasonable fear.

I had to overcome that if I was to survive in a field in which accessibility is as important as visibility. If I didn't start accepting invitations, the invitations would stop coming and that isn't a good thing for someone in the media. The first gig I agreed to was mastering the ceremonies for the Miss Holland pageant and for four weeks leading up to the event, I was certain I couldn't live through it. But, even though I sweated through two tuxes that evening, it wasn't as bad as I feared. I didn't embarrass myself or ruin the evening for the uptight young contestants.

The word was out then and I was off and running, hitting the creamed-peas-and-toast-points circuit with a vengeance. There wasn't a lodge hall, service club, or church basement that wasn't on the itinerary and though I didn't have anything of great importance to say, people seemed to appreciate my showing up and giving them an excuse to charge for the event.

In time, I received a call from the marketing guys at Meijer, inviting me to help them launch a new community service project that came to be called Meijer Community Parties. Though I could use the extra income (television doesn't make you rich), I was skeptical that I had the chops to be a stand up entertainer or have the time to do the traveling required. So, they flew me down to Columbus, Ohio, to check out similar events being presented by a major retailer there and it looked like it could be fun. I agreed to participate and they agreed to find others to do the parties I couldn't handle (TV8 sports guy Warren Reynolds was one of them). I was still a little nervous when we started but it went okay.

I was part of the Meijer Community Party project for the next 21 years and during that time, our team alone (eventually there were three) presented almost 1,800 luncheons and dinners for churches, service clubs, schools, arts organizations, and other non-profit groups – events that helped them do an immeasurable amount of good in their communities. The value of all this to Meijer was the goodwill generated by their sponsorship. The company provided the ingredients to feed 150 people, prizes

With Warren Reynolds and Fred Meijer

to be awarded, a nutritionist to manage the meal (Mushroom Delight Beef Stew, Beef Barley Almondine, Rice Florentine – a different menu each season) and me to provide the entertainment. All free. They also furnished the tickets and permitted the group to charge whatever they could get – and keep the money, which often exceeded a thousand bucks.

Characteristically, Meijer's low-key promotional approach was just plain classy. We had the opportunity at every event to shout the Meijer name and product line, but we didn't have to, because the source of that generosity wasn't lost on anybody. And I'm sure their appreciation showed up at the registers. However, those 21 years must have cost the company millions.

As entertainment goes, what I did would hardly have gotten me a season in the Catskills. I told a few mild jokes, bantered with the ladies, introduced my kitchen colleague (Ann Scott, Lorraine Moore, or Diane Eager), handed out some of Fred's famous Purple Cow cards, gave away some prizes, and hit the road back to the studio. I did most of these events between the six and eleven o'clock newscasts, my tires sometimes barely touching the road, depending on how far afield we were. More than 130,000 miles overall, usually following directions supplied by a member of the hosting group. There were some bad winter nights when it was a little hard to find the silo or the red Chevy pickup where I was supposed to turn.

The Meijer Community Party project was retired in the late 90s as the company developed new and better and more varied ways to assist and support organizations. There's no guessing how much Fred's little grocery chain has contributed to its mission of practical community service.

The Meijer parties and all those rubber chicken dinner speeches might not have seemed as glamorous as being on television, but they were immensely important in bringing me closer to people and the good things they were doing. I'm glad I overcame my reluctance to do personal appearances, and I look back now with genuine pleasure on all those church basement evenings.

There would be 772 more

Somebody straighten that candle

Buckese

Somewhere in all the zillion words I've put on paper through the years is a little diatribe on the obstacles facing any newcomer to our shores in learning our unique language. The many words with similar spellings but differing pronunciations or, worse, identical spellings with different pronunciations and meanings, must be an awful discouragement to anyone seeking to fit into our society. Through and cough. Lose and loose. *Close and close!*

Not that it's any easier for us to learn the intricacies of other languages with their funny demands on lips and tongue. Try French, for example. My wife and I took a YMCA evening course in French many years ago (*we can't remember why*) and all we got out of it was a friendship with the instructor, a charming Frenchwoman, and her husband. Before that, I may have set a record for the number of semesters spent trying unsuccessfully to become familiar with Spanish.

With all that, you would think I am content to speak my native tongue, especially since I made a living using it in public. Mostly, I am. But into our house there has crept an alternate language. I just discovered that some years ago my wife wrote about this affliction when she was taking a Toastmasters course at Grand Valley. I'm only mildly offended.

"As you know, I'm married to a man who has made communication his career. He'd make a lousy Toastmaster, though (*excuse me?*) with his 'and ums.' Yet he's always been very popular (*I'll take that as an apology*) as the weatherman and talk show host, after dinner speaker and emcee. His success flies in the face of all the rules but I believe his sincerity, believability, and, most of all, his wit (*pile it on, Baby*), are factors in his success – ordinary people identify with his 'and ums' (*remember, her words, not mine*). We have a unique language at our house – spoken by only one of us and mostly understood and always appreciated by the other. I call it 'Buckese.' He simply changes word endings in the most unexpected way. For example, 'alleviate' becomes 'allevi-ize'. 'Consolidate,' becomes 'consolidize.' Or he'll add syllables, as in 'removilate' for 'remove.' 'Close' becomes 'closify.' 'Dripilate' for 'drip.' After 36 (*now 55*) years of such nonsense, I'm still amused by it – except in the morning when I can least cope with anything, let alone ridiculosity……...Oh, good grief."

I've changefied her in so many ways.

Day Stalker

Tiger cat, I see you there, across the living room,
Paws tucked in upon the couch, observing through the gloom –
Fixing me with eyes that see just what they want to see.
What primal instinct guided you to share so much with me?

Your jungle world of Meow Mix and Tidy Cat and treats
Might dull the senses of a creature born to hunt live meats.
Yet, here you are, in stalking feet with radar ears aloft,
Waiting for the tell-tale signs of human going soft.

Your kitten days of strings and spools and legs to squeeze between
Are things you seem ashamed of now that you are long and lean.
But when you sit and stare at me like that, you need to know
That when you hunt me in my house, then you will have to go.

Words

I like puzzles. Most of my life has been a puzzle, anyway, so this is no surprise. Whether those little bent naily things that won't come apart or the little balls that won't go in the holes in the glass box or the mental ones that show up on "Brain Games," I enjoy them all – and I'm not intimidated by my failures at solving them. Jigsaw puzzles are fun, too, though I haven't attempted one since I discovered the missing pieces had passed through my dog's digestive tract.

I'm pretty good with those word-search things in the AARP magazine, too, even though I think it's unfair to expect me to find a 27-letter word printed diagonally backwards. But the puzzles that most puzzle me are aptly called CROSSWORDS. I am known to utter many cross words while trying to read the minds of the diabolical lexicographers who must chuckle mightily while thumbing through their dusty libraries for words no modern human could possibly know. In fact, I think there's clear evidence that some of these people aren't familiar with the English language at all, given their sometimes absurd clues that seem unrelated to the words they're calling for.

Not even with the help of my handy little electronic Franklin Spelling Ace am I able to come out ahead. Am I that dumb? More likely the puzzle-meisters are just trying to make me feel inferior by using words that have never appeared anyplace in my life experience. I mean really – I know that a NAP is a siesta and that a NAG is a horse, but how the heck am I supposed to know that a NARD is a fragrant ointment? Think about it. You know that a MAP is a geographical chart and any native Michigander knows that MARL is a natural white clay – but did you know that a MEW is a seagull?

We know what HELL is and we know that a HALO might help us avoid it. But I'll bet you don't know that HEBE is the name of the goddess of youth. For that matter, who knew about NORMA, the divine Teutonic Goddess? Well, come to think of it, I might have seen her in a sideshow once while I was in the Air Force overseas.

I try to look on the bright side in the face of this overwhelming evidence that I'll never be welcome at a Mensa meeting. And I may not know the word when it's called for in a puzzle – but I do try to learn it and remember it. There, however, is the rub. I rarely do, even though crossword authors are as redundant as they are cruel. I wish I had a buck for every time I've forgotten that a mine entrance is an ADIT.

It doesn't trouble me that my wife, a crossword puzzle addict, sticks with it until she's finally conquered the worst of them, no matter how long it takes. It's in her nature to rise above the challenges of life, such as spending more than fifty years with me.

The ultimate humiliation, however, was once watching my brother-in-law do one of those *New York Times* jobs – from 1 across to 150 down – during breakfast, *with a ball point pen.*

My sister and I both married well.

Six Degrees

Long ago, it became evident that earth people are much more connected than they think. This "degrees of separation" thing is real, believe me. I keep falling over it all the time.

A while ago, at some gathering of the movers and shakers, where I was the hired introducer, my wife and I sat at the head table with the distinguished speaker, doing small talk over the creamed peas on toast points. During the course of the dinner, we discovered that many years ago, we'd both worked at the Pentagon at the same time. Of course, I was a 17-year-old summer temp and he was Deputy Director of Military Intelligence – but there we were, working in the same cavernous building, unaware that we were destined to dine together in the far distant future.

Back when I was producing and hosting my morning television show, a very talented young couple were booked to sing. They were an instant hit with the audience and came back to perform several times. We became good friends, but when the show was cancelled and I eventually left the station, we lost touch. Years later, my wife and I moved out of the city and settled into a home in farm country. Having breakfast one Saturday morning at the village café, we were surprised to run into our musical friends. In catching up on each other's lives, we discovered that their farm backed up to our property. We'd been neighbors and didn't know it.

When I was a boy in Maryland, my grandfather used to take me on adventures on the lower Potomac in his big rowboat or in his wheezy old motorboat. After he died, when his place was sold and the old motorboat was headed for the boneyard, I removed its brass running lights and the bronze manufacturer's plate from the engine as reminders of those cider-sweet days on the river with Grandpa. The brass lanterns have been a part of our household décor ever since but the engine nameplate was misplaced until a couple of years ago. When it surfaced, I read the wording on it and discovered that the old one-lung motor that used to propel Grandpa's boat was built by the Regal Gasoline Engine Company in Coldwater, Michigan – the birthplace of the girl I would marry forty years later!

But, wait! There's more. During the mid-fifties, when I was host of an all-night music show on Detroit's clear-channel WJR, a woman wrote and asked about a piece of music I'd played. I wrote back to tell her it was a recording by the Roger Wagner Chorale. Many years later, when my wife and I were clearing out her mother's things after her death, we discovered a copy of that record album, on the back of which she'd written about having bought it because she'd learned about it from a Detroit disc jockey – me!

Five years later, I had met and married her daughter.

Small world hardly covers it.

I Am Mr. Thelma Matthews

My wife denies it every time I say it, but that's who I was – and was happy to be – in certain circles during my Grand Rapids broadcast years. By chance, I married a talented, confident woman who was never in my shadow. It's not easy being married to someone whose line of work carries with it a degree of celebrity. Many show business wives end up leaving their husbands – or killing them – because they feel overwhelmed by their husband's notoriety.

Not so Thelma Irene Ellinger Matthews.

Early in our time in River City, after I'd begun to make personal appearances, she would sometimes accompany me when I went to do a dinner speech. During the usual schmooze time before dinner, she'd sometimes find herself being edged out of the little group around me. I'd do my best to draw her back in but it didn't always work. One evening I lost track of her and feared she'd gone back to the car to wait. But she hadn't. More socially adept than I, she'd become the center of attention of another group across the room.

When we met in Jackson, both working at WILX-TV, she was already a bit of a celebrity herself, the vocalist with the Jackson Civic Band. Her opportunities to perform expanded greatly in Grand Rapids. She became a charter member of the Grand Rapids Symphonic Choir and appeared in almost twenty productions presented by the Calvin Alumni Players, Civic Theatre, and Opera Grand Rapids. For several years, she and our daughter, also gifted with a lovely voice, appeared at festivals and fairs as the folksinging duo "Cornsilk."

I earned the name, "Mr. Thelma Matthews," because as she became involved in the activities of organizations in the community - Women's Committee of the Grand Rapids Symphony, St. Cecilia Music Society, Zonta Club (a term as president), Festival of the Arts - she never felt the need to tell people that I was her husband.

Marg Ed Conn once wrote of her in *Grand Rapids Magazine,* "She has carved her own niche as Thelma Matthews and doesn't trade on her husband's fame. It would probably be fair to say that she's married to a nice man who just happens to be a prominent television figure, rather than a prominent television figure who happens to be her husband. It keeps the family in balance."

It's always been as much fun for me as for her when someone would say, "Oh, *that's* who you're married to." And, not infrequently, someone would say the same thing to me.

Many Hands

Having your face hung out for all to see carries with it certain responsibilities and opportunities to do more than just show up for work and carry home a paycheck. I know few people in our craft who don't consider community service part of their job. A perfect example is my late colleague, Warren Reynolds. In his 35 years at TV8, he and his wife, Sharron, raised millions of dollars for charitable causes. An annual charity golf tournament still bears his name.

Being visible as we were, we were often able to direct our involvement toward things that were of interest to us personally. In no order of importance, my own interests included the arts, community development, history, folk music, and board games. To some degree, I've managed to get involved with all of them during more than 50 years in River City.

Festival '74 souvenir album

I was privileged to serve on the boards of the West Michigan Opera Association and the Grand Rapids Symphony, served a term as president of the Arts Council of Greater Grand Rapids, and was co-chair with Lois Poppen of the 1974 Festival of the Arts. I was honored to be appointed to Mayor Lyman Parks' Downtown Development Study Committee. In 1980, Jack Loeks (the movie guy) and I co-chaired the Grand A-Fair, the business and industry exposition that was part of the opening of Grand Center, the city's new convention and entertainment facility.

I also had the opportunity to serve on committees for St. Cecilia, the Grand Rapids Public Museum, the Muscular Dystrophy Association, and the Grand Rapids Folklore Center. I joined with a bunch of goofy friends who loved board games and didn't mind dressing like butlers, to found the Greater Grand Rapids Great Gatsby Group, which put on annual charity Monopoly tournaments. It was great fun and we managed to help out some worthy causes.

One of the joys of living in the Greater Grand Rapids area, for all of us, is that there is no limit to the ways we can be involved and the good we can do. Not so in many other countries, as Jan Blaich, former director of the Women's Resource Center and president of the Arts Council, learned while she and her husband, Bob, were living in Europe. Volunteering is practically unheard of there because the government does everything.

One of my former TV colleagues who left for a higher paying, higher visibility job in Chicago, told me on his first visit back here that one of the most glaring differences between Grand Rapids and the Windy City was not size or opportunity. "In Grand Rapids," he said, "one person can make a difference."

It's one of River City's distinguishing characteristics that almost everyone who winds up living here is compelled, by the sheer love of the place, to do something to make it better. Every pair of hands that reaches out to help someone, join a cause, contribute time or money, or gets sweaty and dirty helping to build a Habitat house, is making it an even better place.

Aren't we lucky there was room for us here?

Bell

A Story

In his town, he was the go-to guy, always ready to help when asked and never saying no to any request. He seemed not to have a life of his own, for his time seemed always to be filled with activity on someone else's behalf. It was, it seemed to some, his occupation. If he wasn't fixing some old person's broken appliance, or mowing the lawn for someone in the hospital, or helping unload a neighbor's groceries, he could be found tossing the ball with a lonely kid.

His name was Bell. Just Bell. No first name, no middle initial, no Mr. Bell to anybody, young or old. Some of the mothers of young children in the town thought he was creepy and told their kids to avoid him, but the fathers weren't worried and often countermanded their wives' advice.

Nobody knew where he came from. Nobody knew how old he was – not even the postman who delivered his mail and could be counted on to know everything about everyone else in town. Like the town drunk or the village idiot, he was just always there – though he was not either of those things. And though he never went to church, his faith seemed evident, for he could be seen reading his Bible every morning in good weather on his front porch.

Generally, people returned his kindnesses with friendly good will, the older ladies sometimes leaving cakes or pies or cookies on his porch swing – and never failing to identify the sources – just so their plates or tins would find their way home.

But, as is the case so often with those who are giving and thoughtful, people gradually began to take the old man for granted. They assumed he would show up when needed because he always did. Maybe that was creepy after all. Nobody ever had to say, "Go find Bell" when a crisis arose. The crises and Bell always seemed to go hand-in-hand. Some people even suspected that, like the pyromaniac fireman who set fires so he could put them out, maybe Bell had a hand in things that went wrong.

The truly thoughtless and uncaring in town regarded Bell with derision, the result of his oft-spoken promise to take care of the town and its people after he was gone. "These little jobs are just down-payment," he would say. "Something special is in store for everybody here." Others in town, down on their luck or just greedy, liked the sound of it and hoped for the best. Some even went so far as to ask for hints about the size of his account at the bank. But there was no account at the town bank, and nobody knew where he kept his money – not even the no-accounts who broke into his house while he was off helping someone out of a jam. No safe, no box in the closet, no canvas bag under the bed.

But they knew he had money. He bought necessities for people who couldn't afford them; he contributed to good causes; he drove a good car, paid for in crisp new bills; his clothes were anything but shabby. Bell had it, all right, and some fine day they were going to get a piece of it.

Then, one day it happened. They found Bell lying on his porch with his Bible clutched to his chest, his face contorted in pain. They rushed him to the hospital, where the doctors declared he would not survive another day. The word spread that old Bell, that good man who loved his town and cared for its people, was leaving them. There was, then, genuine sorrow among those whose lives he'd touched. They gathered in front of the hospital and prayed for his survival.

And he did survive – that day. And the next. And the day after that. The doctors still said he would die, and soon, but no longer predicted how soon. The weeping in town abated and the sorrow turned to curiosity, then impatience. Too bad about old Bell, that good man. But what about his promise of something special for the town and its good people? Almost everybody in town wondered about this and a few of them felt guilty about that kind of wondering.

One evening, the subject actually came up at the town meeting, when a member of the Council suggested they consider some of those back-burner projects that might now be accomplished, depending on the size of the gift from Bell. Before the meeting was over, the Council had established a subcommittee to consider how best to use the "Bell Gift." Nobody knew where it would be coming from or how much it would be, but as there is safety in numbers, so is there confidence in committees, and nobody left that meeting doubting that the old man was all that stood between them and a substantial shot in the budget.

Another committee came into being around that time. Bell's heart, though damaged beyond repair, soldiered on, keeping the old man alive but sleeping peacefully in his hospital bed, attached to the world only by tubes and wires and monitors. Finally, the doctors came to realize that Bell was their first case of a patient no longer alive but not yet ready to die. He'd been a charity case because no insurance papers were found among his things. They needed the bed, the patient was not ready to relinquish it, so he needed to be moved to a long term care facility. But there was no such thing in the community. The closest thing to long term care was a boarding house run by a retired school bus driver.

The women of the community decided that they would take responsibility for raising the money to upgrade a lower floor room in the boarding house and care for poor old Bell themselves. And so they did. Working in shifts, they gave their time to sit with him and keep the drips going and see to his bodily needs and comforts under the guidance of a rotation of young doctors and nurses. They became a home-grown, unofficial Hospice, calling themselves Bell's Belles.

The hopelessness and burden of their well-meant endeavor wore thin in time and the novelty of it gradually wore off. It seemed a useless waste of time to constantly monitor a person who was no longer a person and even they began to speculate on what would happen when, finally, the great heart beat its last. There were even some in town who thought it would be worthwhile – merciful even – if the ladies just happened to help the old man take his final step across the great threshold into the afterlife.

Compassion faded and died in the town, even as old Bell did not. And so was born the idea of a bell for Bell. Distasteful as it was, the town tinkerer – a man less given to charity than was Bell – was hired to install an alarm system in the old man's boarding house room, connected to the machines that monitored his heartbeat and his respiration. The new routine would consist of a brief daily visit to assure that the machinery was working and the bell was operational. Then, if and when the alarm sounded, the Bell's Belle on standby at the time would go to the old man's side to make sure the ghost was given up.

Secretly, every living soul in town listened for the bell that would, at last, signal the release of the Bell Gift, the largesse that would wash over them all and change their lives forever.

Many months passed. A year. Then one glorious crimson and gold day in Autumn, the bell rang and the Bell's Belle on standby – as well as every other woman who wore the Bell's Belles T-shirt – rushed to the bedside, accompanied by almost everybody else in town, all wanting to be sure it wasn't a false alarm. It wasn't. Old Bell had finally gone over to the other side.

Well, the crowd dispersed and euphoria swept through the town like a flood. People laughed who never laughed. People prayed who never prayed. Then, suddenly, it was quiet. They looked at each other in confusion and disappointment – even a faint touch of guilt – as they waited for something to happen. Day by day, their mood changed and a sort of community meanness arose. People swore who never swore. They came to believe that they'd been had. That creepy old man who had his nose in everybody's business all those years had pulled a monumental fast one on them.

Bell's body was laid in a common grave without ceremony. Nobody showed up to grieve, though an anonymous donor did have a stone placed. It said, simply, "Bell – A Good Man."

When the Town Council met the next time, there was a buzz of excitement as the chairman placed a small, brass-bound mahogany box on the table. "Boys, there may yet be a reason to celebrate. I found this box on my porch this morning when I went out for the paper." Carved into the top of the box was BELL, the name they'd once loved, then hated, now appreciated again. A breathless hush fell over the room as the chairman carefully raised the lid and removed a manila envelope, from which he extracted an engraved certificate. Written in a strong hand, were the words, "This box contains everything you did for me while I was among you, returned in full."

It took a long while for the town to return to normal. Bell's Belles and a couple of the volunteer doctors quietly dismantled the room at the boarding house, returning it to rentable condition. The Town Council revised the list of pending projects and gave consideration to adopting new policies regarding gifts to the community. The small, brass-bound mahogany box was put on display at the town library for a short time, after which it disappeared.

And, soon enough, people forgot it ever existed.

After all, it was empty.

Armed and Ridiculous

As much as I worry about the American romance with firearms and the mischief, both criminal and accidental, their presence allows, I must admit to some serious conflict of interest. Although I favor the administration of fair and efficient control of gun ownership, I understand the concern of those who fear that registration might somehow restrict their right to own them.

Now, let's get that Second Amendment argument out of the way right now. The "right to bear arms" clause was written at a time when much of the nation was wilderness and people needed the means to protect and feed themselves. They also needed the freedom to band together as militia to defend their communities and their young country. Unfortunately, there's no way to persuade a very large segment of today's population that their elected government is capable of providing that service and has no intention of seizing their weapons in doing so. Their very vocal national organization, funded largely by firearms manufacturers, is more convincing.

Enough of that. I have been where they are. As a boy, one of my proudest possessions was a pair of Colt-style cap pistols with fake pearl handle grips embossed with a longhorn skull and tooled leather holsters and belt with a big, silver horseshoe buckle. I never lost a gunfight.

When I became a member of the Washington, DC, High School Cadet Corps, the armories had been stripped of weapons for the war effort, so my first experience with a long gun was a wooden replica, useful only in practicing the manual of arms. After the war, we were issued surplus 1903 .30 caliber Lee-Enfield bolt-action rifles, which were wonderful for rifle drills but useless for shooting each other, because the pins had wisely been removed.

I finally got my hands on a device capable of putting a hole through something when I arrived in Korea and the Air Force issued me a .30 caliber, semi-automatic M1 carbine. As a ground radio operator, I didn't need it, but we were all armed in case the base was overrun before the Mounties could save us. We used them like toys, wasting ammunition shooting at cans and rocks and trees like kids. It was a very sweet piece – but the peaceful South Koreans thought we were lunatics.

After I came back and was safely into my broadcasting career in Detroit, a truck driver pal who was a hunter and a range shooter, persuaded me to get into the fun. So I bought a very nice Smith and Wesson .38 caliber Combat Masterpiece revolver and blew the brains out of many a straw target at the Pontiac Police range. Much fun and the good feeling of owning a weapon. After I married and moved to Grand Rapids, I took some comfort in knowing that on a shelf in the bedroom closet, I had the means to defend my family if the need ever arose.

Then, one sunny day, I came down with a serious case of common sense and knew that the gun on the shelf in the closet was more likely to cause one of my children to shoot me than it was to scare off any intruders. Even if I'd had it in a gun safe, it was unlikely the bad guys would wait while I went to get it. So, I invited the Grand Rapids police chief to be a guest on my morning show and we talked about the problems our loose gun laws might be causing. Then I handed over my very nice .38 caliber Smith and Wesson Combat Masterpiece and went home feeling safer than I'd felt since I single-handedly settled the West with my pearl-handled cap pistols.

Home Improvement

My wife thinks I'm having an affair because I so often come home with a smile on my face. More often than not, it's because I've been to Menard's, the home improvement joint, taking advantage of their almost monthly 11% off sale. Never 10 or 12 – always 11%. There has to be a marketing consultant loose in the home improvement business.

I'll admit that few experiences in life so entrance me as just standing in the middle of one of those nuts and bolts warehouses. Most intelligent adults only get that feeling in banks and bakeries, but I grew up in a family of carpenters and cabinetmakers, for whom the smell of lumber competed with the aroma of fried chicken as the essence of life. I only wish my father could have lived long enough for just one visit to such hardware heaven.

In his day, gathering the ingredients for the job was a lot like shopping in countries where the meat and the bread are found in separate shops. I remember going with him to the lumberyard and the hardware store for materials, places that evoked similar shivers of ecstasy. That was when your neighborhood hardware store had everything you needed to keep your house in order. And the guy behind the counter knew all there was to know about how to use what you were buying, in case you weren't my Dad. You needed it, he had it. No waiting for the next boat from China and none of that stuff about parts no longer being available.

Nostalgia aside, I have to admit that these big building supply boxes have something going for them. What tarnishes it a bit for me, though, is having some earnest young clerk ask, "Are you finding what you need?" when you know he's praying that my answer will be, "Yes," because it's as certain as sunrise that if I ask him how to remove a frozen back-threaded three-quarter by six-inch brass carriage bolt, he won't even know what that is. He'll just turn pale and run off to find the department manager, who's on break until nightfall.

I'll give them this, however. Those young guys know the store layout. Ask where the drinafeens and transaframs are and any one of them can lead you smartly right to them. They won't know what they are or how to install them, but they do keep traffic from backing up in the aisles.

And that, sadly, is a problem your neighborhood hardware dealer never had to face.

Flivvers

At the time I'm writing this, my personal vehicle is a 17-year-old Chevrolet Malibu with more miles on it than the International Space Station. It is my vehicle of choice and I love every blemish on its once-beautiful body and every strange noise under the hood. We are much alike in that regard and I believe it loves me none the less. In truth, I just happen to like old cars.

I suppose it's not very good for my image, given the expectation of most people that anyone in my racket should be tooling around in something new, bright, and classy. Some of my broadcast colleagues, more status-conscious than I am, had wheels that were worth the extra attention they drew in the parking lot. I just felt more comfortable driving something my father would have liked and wouldn't cause me great anguish if someone parked too close and dinged the door.

The first car I owned was a 1929 Ford Model A Cabriolet I bought while I was a freshman at Ohio Wesleyan University. On a hardship scholarship, I could hardly afford such a luxury, but it was only twenty-five bucks and gas was seventeen cents a gallon and I was already wise enough to know you only live once. "Murgatroyd," as I called it, wasn't pretty but it ran

Murgatroyd

like a sewing machine and it was reliable enough for me to drive home to Washington and back once without any trouble. I made a ten-dollar profit when I sold it to another student, but I still have the Ohio license plate. It was only a coincidence that the numerals were BM – 67.

In another coincidence, my second car (relax – I won't list them all), which I didn't acquire until nearly five years later, was an almost exact duplicate of the first one. Purchased from a fellow airman at Selfridge Air Force Base after I returned from Korea, it looked as bad and ran as well as the first one. This one didn't get a name but it did get bold lettering painted on the door - "Tops at the Top of Your Radio Dial – WSDC – 1590" – a hint that I was doing something besides defending Democracy. That one cost me four times as much as the first one, but I was a little better off as a Staff Sergeant than I had been as a student.

Then came my first *new* car. My heart still flutters just thinking about it. Was it bright and classy, now that I had my first job in radio? Not on your life. It was a dark blue (Air Force influence) 1953 Chevy sedan delivery – a commercial utility model similar to a station wagon without the extra side doors and windows and no back seat. It was a practical choice because I put bedding in the back so I could sleep in it when travelling.

Many cars have followed, all of them Chevrolets because that was the car my father trusted most. In fact, when he died, he got his last ride to Arlington National Cemetery in a Chevrolet hearse because the funeral director's Cadillac had been wrecked the day before his funeral. If we hadn't known him better, we might have thought Pop had a hand in that.

When we arrived in Grand Rapids, one of my early assignments at TV8 was to participate in the coverage of the famous Woodland Antique Automobile Tour. We didn't have an antique car ourselves, so we rode along with Bud and Lorene Jonas of Belding in one of their many cars. We had so much fun that we decided to join the Horseless Carriage Club, the co-sponsor of the event, even though the only thing we owned that had anything to do with old cars was a set of seat covers for a 1918 Hupmobile I'd picked up at a flea market. I thought they helped me fit in. (A couple drove all the way from southern Indiana to buy those from us.)

Because our interest in antique cars grew steadily, I decided to produce a documentary on the subject. "The Greasy Pioneers" included interviews with West Michigan collectors and footage of their cars and associated materials. One of those people was west side used car dealer Vic Johnson, who owned a rare Grand Rapids-built Continental (not the fancy Lincoln version that came later.) He also had a well-worn 1931 Chevrolet Sport Sedan, with which I fell in love after driving it in one scene. He sold it to me for $600, allowing me to pay 50 bucks a month for it.

Then it was all in for us. With the help of some of the guys who were in the documentary, I slowly restored the car and we drove it in many parades and took it to several old car meets. Even though we almost lost it in the 1967 tornado, we got it back into shape in time to put lots of brass on the mantelpiece that year, including a Best-of-Show trophy.

That car is now somewhere in Ohio or Indiana, and we've been out of the old car hobby for many years, though we haven't entirely lost our connections. The year I left television, I produced a documentary – "Treasure at Hickory Corners" – about the amazing Gilmore Car Museum at Hickory Corners, near Richland, Michigan. Anyone who's ever had a thing for old cars should spend some time, as we sometimes do, wandering through its huge collection of vintage and classic motor vehicles and automotive memorabilia, housed in historic Michigan barns and its big new Heritage Center. The place is, truly, a Michigan treasure - and a mecca for guys like me.

Pride and joy

Attentive Driving

Back when I was working fulltime and free-lancing the rest of the time, I was on the road as much as your average Fuller Brush man (the only one left, in California), which is why the odometer numbers on my seventeen-year-old Malibu are wearing out. Fortunately, I love to drive. Even more fortunately, they still *let* me drive, though I'd rather have my teeth filled than drive on ice.

In my maturing years, I've come to be more patient behind the wheel. While I still get steamed at the stupidity of other drivers, I haven't had a good case of road rage since about thirty years ago when some yahoo ran me into the median on the Ford Freeway. I chased him across town until I cut somebody else off and realized that I was just as big a jerk as he was. Now when something like that happens, I just smile and hope he meets a State Trooper having a bad day.

Having driven on many long trips, I'm familiar with the worst road hazard of all – boredom. When I was still driving an average of a hundred fifty miles a day, I'd sometimes get lost in fantasy and lose track of where I was – or, worse, fall asleep. I discovered a remedy for the latter at a rest stop on the New York Thruway: chunky coffee-flavored lozenges that tasted like car tires and had so much caffeine in them they made your eye lids fly up like window shades. They didn't cure boredom, however. So, I invented a little game I call, "The Perfect Ride." It closely resembles what NASCAR drivers do but without the speed. I rarely drive above the speed limit, anyway, because I don't need to get there ahead of everybody else anymore. Besides, in a car as old as mine, speeding is right up there with tap dancing on land mines.

"The Perfect Ride" game (patent pending) consists of merely straightening out the road, trying to time my progress so precisely that I can always have the inside lane on curves (this only works on expressways, by the way) and never have to drop out of cruise control. This may sound simple, possibly a little stupid, but it's all but impossible to make it all the way to your destination without having to relinquish the preferred lane to faster or slower drivers. Dumb as this may seem, it keeps my mind clear, my eyes open, and my hands steady on the wheel.

And there's a practical side to this game. By straightening out the road in this way, I actually drive fewer miles, get there sooner, save gas, and reduce wear and tear on my tires. Well, you may ask, how much shorter does that make the trip? I wondered that, too, so I clocked the mileage on my commute to Blue Lake Public Radio. Would you believe that by simply always taking the inside lane on curves on what was then an eighty-mile round trip I saved – are you sitting down? – six-tenths of a mile! At that rate, I will have to buy one less set of tires in my lifetime – if I live to be a hundred and forty years old.

Hey, you gotta save where you can.

When Our Daughter Ran Away

1970 and 1983

It was about 6:45 PM on a chilly March evening when our beloved older child, the daughter whose very existence was a miracle because she was nearly killed by a dog two years earlier, ran away. At the customary age of six-going-on-seven, she wrote her first declarative message to us: "Dear Mom and Dad: I am going to away run."

And away run she did. That disorganized streak, whose usual reaction to crisis was melodrama, prepared to leave with an efficiency not seen since she was born. With a running commentary on her reason for going (we were mean to her), she dragged her suitcase from the attic; packed a Sunday dress, favorite comic book, and pillow; filled a plastic bag with survival rations (three slices of bread, a pack of gum, two caramels, two Tootsie Rolls, and a piece of fish left from the last meal she intended to share with us); counted her money ($2.27 in a pink plastic purse); dressed in warm clothes; kissed her mother, brother, and me – and walked out of our lives.

We could not have been more casual as she prepared to leave, merely offering comments on the time and the temperature. She declined our offer to contribute to her funds. Only her mother accompanied her to the door and asked her not to go. Her brother said he didn't care – he'd find someone else to play with – and I sat "reading" the newspaper in the living room.

No frontier village posted sentries faster than did our house when the door closed. Her mother from the kitchen and I from the living room, watched her struggle with the suitcase down the long driveway, pausing now to look back at the house, now to rest the suitcase, now to consider her progress, now to switch hands – and she was getting harder to see in the quickening dusk.

I had a better view of her from the garage, but it wasn't good enough. She was nearly to the road, a tenth of a mile farther than I'd expected her to go – farther than she would have been allowed to go if she'd asked – beyond the limit I had established in a bargain with God. I walked down the driveway after her. I could see her standing by the road as the first car passed and I walked faster. Then another car passed and still I thought I saw her there. But she was not there when I got to the end of the driveway. A third car stopped about 50 yards away, then drove off. I've never felt such cold, sickening panic.

Her voice from the field across the road was like Christmas morning. "Hi, Daddy. Did you walk down for the paper?" *Thank you, God!*

Casual again, I crossed the road and offered to carry her suitcase. She thought that would be nice but only if it meant across the field and not back up the driveway. What I said to her then - about the loneliness of the world and the warmth and love and familiar things waiting for her return – neither of us can remember now. I'm sure I thought that if I was so poorly prepared to outwit a child of six-going-on-seven, how would I deal with the real crises yet to come?

But we did walk back together, hand in hand, leaning into that biting March wind – and I did carry her suitcase.

Thirteen years later, the suitcase would go down the driveway again. That time, it didn't come back. Her need to be free of us never really disappeared. When she was willing to accept love and affection, we were overjoyed, probably in itself off-putting. It wasn't that she didn't love us. It was just expressed in measured doses so as not to interfere with the low-level combat that accompanied her through the house. It was sad to see, that pointless battle with her environment. And, of course, it wasn't who she was elsewhere. A good student with an outgoing personality, the rest of the world saw a different girl. The problem must have been us.

Well, me. I thought it unreasonable that she was not born with my sense of logic. The unspoken message she heard was be cute, not child-like. Her mother walked the tightrope between us, buying time for me to grow up. By the time I came to know the mistake I'd made, she was a young adult and my white flag was suspect.

So, she left. No foot-of-the-driveway negotiation. This time we knew there was more for her out there on her own than in that state of arrested development common to all children who stay too long at home. We helped her go, then stood in the doorway of her room and looked at the landfill clutter that settled in her wake – all the stuff that conspires to stave off adulthood. The long-abandoned bedtime prayers, the goodnight songs, the exorcised boogeymen, the time outs, the door slamming – all would permeate the atmosphere long after she'd gone.

For twenty turbulent years we gave her everything we thought she needed and did what we could to guide her to independence. But we – I – never quite gave her what she had to leave home to discover. The wonder of it all is that now she is sharing with us, in full measure, what she found.

It's called happiness.

Three O'Clock

(For teachers and daycare providers everywhere)

Zippered, muffled, snapped and buckled,
Shiny faces by the door,
Looking like the crew at Houston,
Just before the rocket's roar.

Socked and booted, gloved and rooted
By the eyeballs to the clock,
Ready, steady, poised and waiting
For their daily freedom shock.

Smarter than they were this morning,
Drinking deep from Learning's joys,
Mother, Dads, and siblings waiting
For this avalanche of noise.

Once Upon a Time

He sees his sweetest, clearest visions
In the eyes of little children
Playing games he used to play
When he was them.

Going Straight

Our second born was the quiet one. While our daughter was independent and determined to set her own course early on, our son was rarely troublesome. They were both just normal kids, saddled with parents painfully new at the game. When conflicts arose, we were in charge, but we were careful not to let them see our fear, lest they send us to *our* room.

They were both talented. She was blessed with a beautiful singing voice. He had an unusually observant eye that developed into first-rate design and photographic skills. Some of his photos hang on our walls and I cherish a magazine article he and I produced together on the old Ravenna Flea Market, illustrated with his sensitive photographs. The two of them differed in other ways, though. Our daughter was never in police custody. The quiet one was – twice.

One night during his senior year in high school he did something he came to wish he hadn't done. In the lead-up to senior prank night, he and his classmates conspired to occupy the high school grounds and do silly stuff. Nothing shameful or destructive – just the kind of monkey business that only teenagers would think of doing, to get a rise out of the administration. The occupation wasn't even forbidden. In fact, I think they were told they wouldn't be bothered as long as nothing was broken and no one attempted to enter the school building. You bet.

At about 4:30 in the morning our phone rang, and a polite deputy sheriff suggested we come get our son out of the back seat of his cruiser. Filled with disbelief and anger, we went to the school, expecting to learn that our quiet, intelligent son had broken the law and ruined all of our lives. On arrival, we learned that no crime had been committed and he wasn't under arrest. It turns out he was mostly guilty of bad timing. Some kids had managed to get in and out of the building through an open skylight. So, our pride and joy took a shot at it, too – and dropped right into the arms of a security guard, who hustled him out the front door and turned him over to the deputy. Do you have any idea how difficult it is to drive while trying to keep from laughing out loud?

A year later, a more mature version of the kid in the cruiser was off to Ithaca College to study film making. We watched with pride as he headed down the driveway and into his future, his car stuffed to the windows with the worldly goods that didn't fit in the rented pod on the roof. We looked forward to his phone call telling us he'd arrived safely and was settled in.

It was late in coming and the answer to "How was your trip?" was hardly what we expected. He'd made it to the Canadian border where, for three hours, he waited under the watchful eye of a Mounty while a cadre of customs agents unloaded everything he'd spent two days packing. It's worth mentioning here that during that year between high school and college, our quiet boy had grown a beard and stopped getting haircuts. That worldly look and the stuffed white Camaro pretty much assured the gatekeepers that they were about to make the drug bust of the day.

To his credit, his reaction to this intrusion was calm and philosophical. As he explained it to us, he was actually amused because he knew that when the border patrol finally discovered that his load of contraband was mostly clean underwear, he wouldn't be the one who was embarrassed.

He has since given up his life of crime.

Calamity Charlie

Overall, I'm not a person prone to accidents. I've had a few experiences that bear forgetting but adversity doesn't follow me around like the little dark cloud over the head of the Li'l Abner character with the unpronouncable name. I am, in fact, rather graceful for a guy who never learned to dance. But there've been a few times when people have been glad not to be me.

When our son and three of his college buddies were sharing a house on Long Island while trying to crack the New York comedy market, my wife and I retrieved his worldly goods from storage and rented a truck to take them to him. Our preference had been a 15-foot van, but the rental agency stuck us with a truck so big that, even with all his stuff, we could have held a pep rally in it. Big cab-over-engine job that made us feel like we were piloting an 18-wheeler, good buddy.

We got used to it within a few miles and negotiated the trip with no trouble – until we found ourselves, lost, going 55 miles per hour in the curb lane of the Long Island Freeway (TRUCKS FORBIDDEN) in wall-to-wall, bumper-to-bumper, four-lane Sunday afternoon traffic. Then it got worse. Rounding a curve, we saw ahead an arched stone overpass with clearance marked a foot shorter than the height of the truck and no way to stop or change lanes.

The top of that truck peeled back like a sardine can, scattering bits of plastic and aluminum over the heads of many surprised drivers. Fortunately, we sailed through and quickly found a place to pull off to assess the damage. The truck was still drivable and Chip's goodies were still intact, so there was no reason not to proceed, find a police station to report the incident, and go find the boys. Except we were now off the road on a curve just beyond the overpass with no way to take advantage of any break in traffic to pull out. I did a little walk-around and discovered that we were just below an on ramp so the only alternative to causing another accident was to drive up and over the embankment, and re-enter the freeway via the on ramp, thereby breaking the same anti-truck law again.

The rest of the story is anti-climactic. We delivered the stuff, reported the accident, turned in the truck, and were billed $3,000 for the damage, despite the insurance we'd bought. I'm probably a wanted man in Grapevine, Texas, home of the rental company, because I wrote a letter to the president thereof, telling him in various ways that it would be a cold day in hell before I paid for their stupidity in selling insurance inadequate to cover the dummies who rent their trucks.

And after all that, our kid didn't break into comedy – although he did break into laughter. We're still considering writing him out of the will.

Lost Youth

A Lament

No, not mine. This is about a much greater loss than the disappearance of the first half of my life. I'm concerned about the loss of innocence and possibility and potential of a huge portion of America's youth. The kids who become soiled and spoiled by the circumstances that close in on them before they have a chance to become what their mothers hope for and society expects.

This is on my heart because of something I just learned from doing a little cheap and easy research through the wonder of Googling. What might have taken me a bus trip to the library and an hour of riffling through microfilm when I was a student, I learned in five minutes by just typing in a name and clicking on the first paragraph that popped up on my monitor.

The name – and I want you to say the name aloud as you read this so you won't forget it – is **Rashad Williams**. Go ahead – say it. Now remember it because Rashad William is a classic, unfathomable case of lost opportunity. Not just his. Yours and mine and the nation's.

Rashad Williams was an African-American kid growing up in San Francisco. He was an outstanding track athlete, a better-than-average student, and a thoughtful, loving child to his mother and stepfather, with whom he had a strong bond. Rashad Williams was a young man who knew that life holds promise for those who care about others. His actions proved it.

The massacre at Columbine High School in Littleton, Colorado, in 1999 affected Rashad in a very significant way. He followed the story in the papers and on television and was deeply concerned about the tragic changes in the lives of the students who survived. One in particular touched him. Lance Kirklin received five bullet wounds, one of which required reconstruction of his face. Rashad told his mother he had to do something to help, so he went out and raised $40,000. Then he and his mother flew to Colorado and presented the money to Lance. A bond developed between the two boys, a perfect example of the unlikely giving way to the possible.

This act of generosity and good will made Rashad a celebrity. He appeared on the network morning shows, he was asked to address school groups and professional organizations, and his heartwarming story was told around the world. I told it myself on the radio and ended my remarks with these words: "Rashad Williams will be eligible to run for President in the year 2016. You'd do well to remember his name. I know Lance Kirklin will never forget it."

So, I wondered how Rashad was doing now and how close he might be to throwing his hat in the ring. Here's what I learned: At the age of 21, six years after his remarkable act of generosity, Rashad Williams had dropped out of school, robbed two banks, and was shot dead running from a home invasion. This amazing young man whose potential seemed immeasurable, had fallen from grace and embraced a lifestyle that no one could have predicted.

There's no punchline to this story. Only a deepening sense of frustration and anger over the darkness in our society that is stunting our children. This has nothing to do with race or lack of opportunity or police brutality or broken homes. It has everything to do with the loss of innocence and the squandering of opportunity. I don't know how we can change that. Do you?

The Age of Wonder

My grandson, who played some killer trombone at Blue Lake Fine Arts Camp and in the St. Cecilia Youth Philharmonic, and might have found a seat in a good orchestra, has chosen to lay down the 'bone and pick up the pen. Inasmuch as his mother, his uncle, and his grandparents all have some ink in their blood, you might expect me to feel good about that. And I do – a little. The problem for me is that he's using his talent – and he is a talented poet – to fulfill his dream of being a rap performer. Notice that I don't use "artist" or "musician" with the word "rap." That's because to my elderly ear, there's little that's artistic or musical in the rap genre. As practiced by the successful rappers, it's mostly angry rhymes (and much of that anger directed at women and police) set to a beat. In defense of my grandson, I'll admit that his rhymes are more often spirit-filled and reflective than angry and never vitriolic. Which, I fear, dooms his chances of getting anywhere in a field whose muse is always pissed off.

Or does this just show my age?

A good many years ago – forty, in fact – I wrote a magazine piece entitled, "Rock Radio: Child Abuse Set to Music." I wrote it in righteous rage after hearing my daughter singing along with a recording called "I Wanta Do Somethin' Freaky to You" on the car radio. A criminally suggestive lyric that no 12-year-old child should hear but was on every rock station all day and all night long. And responding to its very intent, the kiddies were going out and buying the 45 RPM record, packaged in its own slick cardboard jacket bearing a photo of two teenagers on a couch, he with his hand inside her sweater. I assure you that one twelve-year-old did not.

We had a family policy about the car radio. My wife and I felt it only fair that each of us should be able to hear some of what he liked while we were travelling, rather than have a mobile standoff or having to listen to cries of "unfair" from the back seat. So, we'd listen to classical or folk music when it was our turn, hoping it might lead the progeny toward good taste, then switch to the rock stations the back seat preferred and hold our tongues while they were entertained by sounds that only vaguely resembled music. And on those rare occasions when something actually appealed to us, we'd score brownie points by saying so.

Then came the day when we were driving to the mall to do some Christmas shopping and the Freaky song freaked me out. I asked her if she knew what she was singing about and was comforted to hear that she just liked the beat. Still, it troubled me that people in my craft were using their stations with such indefensible disregard for the age group that dominated their audience. This festered with me for about a week and then I did something completely out of character for me: I started contacting the general managers of the several rock stations in Grand Rapids to see if I might persuade them to stand up to the record industry and refuse to play such mindless, dangerous crap.

Of the six or seven managers I talked with, only one gave a hint that his conscience told him it was what he should be doing – "But I can't do it alone and I know the others won't go along." He was right. The rest of them told me in various ways to mind my own business. So I wrote the magazine article and embarrassed them not even one little bit. The programing and the lack of responsibility only got worse.

I look back on that episode now and realize how naïve I was to think that change was possible. Stations that were in live-or-die competition with each other for adult listeners who loved the raunchy morning zoo announcers and adolescents who were titillated by the sex-filled music could only have changed if their corporate owners suddenly decided ratings didn't matter, profit was unimportant, and Hell had frozen over.

And as my children would happily tell you now, I was showing my age.

I suppose it's just as well old cranks like me aren't in charge of anything anymore. Long ago we started to sound like our parents, who thought everything we liked foretold the fall of mankind. If I had my way, I'd still take those station managers to the woodshed. I'd also close all the tattoo parlors (I only wish I could live long enough to see some of those butterfly and Jesus-on-the-cross "inks" as they will appear when their wearers reach their dotage). It is most definitely my age that fails to see the beauty in arms and shoulders and necks covered in abstract pastels and anarchist declarations. What happened to the modest "Mother" we used to see on athletes?

And you don't want to hear my opinion on the concerted effort to get kids hooked on e-cigarettes and so-called energy drinks available at your friendly gas station checkout. More and more, I suppose I'm beginning to resemble the old guy in the Jimmy John's spot who asks the fellow delivering his sandwich, "What took you so long?"

Give me a few minutes and I'll think of some more stuff that wrinkles my girdle.

Road Trip

When friends tell me of their trips to far off exotic and historic places, it reminds me that except for the free trips my grateful nation gave me to Japan and Korea, I've never been out of the country – unless you count driving the shortcut across Canada to New England. My wife, on the other hand, the real sophisticate in the family, has done Europe four times.

Going anywhere that requires standing in line and taking off my shoes at an airport is not my idea of having a good time. I enjoy flying; just not the complexities that make it possible. And as for cruises, count me out. I had one round trip, shared with two thousand fellow airmen, the return trip through a full-blown Pacific typhoon (the only fun part of the trip). Enough for me.

But I do love road trips. Years ago, when the kiddies were still small enough to require them to go wherever we went, we used to take motor home trips to folk festivals in New York state. But the kids grew up and our folkie friends grew old, so those trips petered out.

A few years ago, my wife and I decided to go see our son in the DC area, and, instead of flying, to take our time getting there. Well, that was just more fun than people ought to be allowed to have. A couple of thousand miles through the back waters of Ohio, West Virginia, Virginia, Maryland, and back. It was a leisurely, touristy kind of trip, allowing us to appreciate the uniqueness of the villages we came upon – like Hurricane and Nitro and Long Bottom and Wilderness and Pickerington and Spy Run Gap and Pigs Ear and Flinderation. We drove on wide, sweeping Interstates and twisty little two-lanes that barely clung to the sides of mountains.

We explored a coal mine, visited Thomas Jefferson's Monticello, ate in mountaintop inns, rode the Ohio River aboard a paddle wheeler, spent a night with an old college chum, had lunch with a high school friend, and visited my parents' graves in Arlington National Cemetery.

We rediscovered the silly fun of reading the road signs, billboards, and vanity license plates to each other – sometimes in unison. Our favorites were a West Virginia plumbing shop called "Scotty's Potties" and an Ohio license plate inscribed "UB OTAY." We thought we were, too.

It wasn't a Caribbean cruise or a romp on the Riviera. It was just a road trip through what makes this country the envy of the world – the peaceful American Experience. It was wonderful in every way.

The best part, of course, as with any trip to any place, was getting home. If there was a worst part, maybe it was not hearing "Are we there yet?" from the back seat.

The Vacation

A Story

After Bob and Roberta Fieldstone had been married for twelve years, having worked hard to get ahead in the game of life and provide a secure and happy home for their three kids – Frederick, Felicity, and Melvin – they finally felt they could afford a decent family vacation. They'd done the short trips, the overnights, the amusement park visits, but they'd never actually packed up and headed out on a real adventure. Load the old Chevy wagon with all they'd need to survive the long days of driving across the country to some distant, historic destination.

They'd talked about this for some time, lying in bed on warm nights when the ceiling fans were barely providing the comfort necessary to fall into deep sleep. At first it was mere speculation, tempered by the feeling that they couldn't really afford the time away from Bob's sales job commissions. Not a problem for Roberta, who didn't work (Bob would never understand that raising three kids and keeping house for her cheapskate husband was *real* work, unlike what he did all day talking on the phone). But the more they thought about it, the more they felt it was something they deserved for the twelve years they'd devoted to feeding Freddie, Felicity, and Melvin.

God knows, that wasn't easy. Freddie, the oldest at 12, born after a gestation period that was historically brief, was a demanding, intellectual brat, certain from birth that his parents were assigned to him from a pool of social misfits. Felicity, barely weaned at 11, was capable of charming everyone in the world at large, but turned everything expected of her at home into a three-act play. And there was Melvin. Poor Melvin, who escaped an F-name only because Roberta's rich uncle was a Melvin and – well, you know. At 10 years of age, he was the runt of the litter and the only one in the pack who might make it to adulthood without going into foster care. Truth be told, Bob and Roberta (they called each other Bobby) would have preferred escaping their judgmental issue for a week or two, but knew that would not go down well with the neighbors or whoever they could bribe to watch over the little darlings in their absence.

Like all good ideas, this one took many rounds of nocturnal discussion and debate before a decision was reached, a plan was hatched, and a destination chosen. The Fieldstones would head for the Grand Canyon, camping as they went, and hope the exciting, educational experience would make this the year they'd never forget. And so it would be.

They gathered together for a family meeting, a practice that worked while the children were too young to begin plotting the overthrow of civilization. Now, it was all the Bobbies could do to attract their children's attention long enough to herd them into one room without chaos breaking out. Once corralled, it was just as difficult to see all their eyes at one time, engaged as they were in operating the personal communication devices in their hands. Bob couldn't help thinking his offspring were better suited to cells than cell phones.

Roberta opened the negotiations with exactly the wrong words. The three heads all rose in unison as did their response. Never was a two-word phrase spoken with such clarity.

"No way!" they chorused. "Are the two of you nuts?"

Roberta regrouped and looked to her husband for support.

"Look, kids, we don't do anything together as a family anymore and we just think it would do us all good to get out of here and go someplace special for awhile."

Felicity rolled her eyes and immediately started sending blanket texts to her like-minded pals that she might have to call the authorities on her parents, who were clearly guilty of child abuse.

Freddie's response was unexpected, mostly because of his startling announcement that he couldn't be away from summer football practice that long because he'd lose his place on the team. It was unexpected because he'd never been known to pick up a football – or any other object or device employed in sports – in his life. If it didn't come with covers and pages and illustrations, it was of no interest to him.

His siblings and parents snapped to attention. "You're going out for football? When did that happen?"

"The minute Mother came up with that equally absurd suggestion that we imprison ourselves in that wreck of a car for two weeks."

Bob stepped in. "Now, listen, Frederick. There's no reason to disrespect your mother for wanting to make your summer a little more fun. And there's nothing wrong with our car."

"Well, if that's your idea of fun, my disrespect extends to you."

"That's enough. Go to your room."

Felicity responded quickly to that. "Hold it. If he gets to go to his room, I'm going to mine."

"No, you're not. We'll make this decision without your brother. This is still a family meeting."

Melvin, the wise and quiet one, spoke up. "Alright, let's cool down here. Fred, shut up and sit down. Felicity, put that thing away and let's just listen to what they have to say. I think they mean us no harm, so maybe we can get out of this without our lives being ruined."

Roberta looked at her son and wondered where this adolescent wisdom and authority came from. Certainly not her husband, who couldn't influence a light switch.

"Melvin, why don't you run the meeting for us. Maybe your siblings will respond to you better than they do to their *parents*."

"Please don't call me by that name, Mom. You know I hate it. It sounds too Jewish."

"Honey, it's a perfectly good name. And you are half-Jewish you know."

"Come off it, Mom. When was the last time you were in a synagogue? And what good did it do to name me after your Uncle Got-Bucks? He left his money to that home for wayward cats."

Bob sat with his hands in his lap. "Okay, Mel. What would you like us to call you?"

"Melissa."

The silence in the room was so deep and wide, their collective breathing sounded like the wind in treetops.

Felicity looked at her brother as if he'd just broken wind. "Very funny, you jerk."

Freddie, subdued until that moment, gazed with admiration at his brother. "Excellent!"

Roberta's shock was evident. "Mellie, what are you saying?"

"I'm saying you've been dressing me wrong for ten years. I'm a girl and I want to be treated like one. And from now on, my name is Melissa."

Several days later, when the four survivors returned home from Bob's funeral, there was a decidedly different atmosphere in the Fieldstone family home. The children were newly respectful of their mother, who'd handled the double loss of her husband and her son, now a girl, with courage and caring for their own shock and grief. After all, Bob had been a good husband and father, who wanted the best for each member of his family, of whom he was proud. That the shock of learning his progeny consisted of two girls and a boy instead of two boys and a girl was too much for him didn't make him a bad person. Just a dead one.

Roberta, in her new role as a single parent, rose to new heights as a loving mother, successful in guiding her three children to adulthood. The boyfriend who eventually came into her life, an ophthalmologist, bought her a new car every other year.

Freddie graduated cum laude from Harvard and had a distinguished career in science. The Frederick Fieldstone texts on space technology are still widely studied. He never married.

Felicity developed into a brilliant and beautiful young woman, earned a law degree and spent her career defending the rights of helpless people. She remained single.

Melvin, who soon grew tired of wearing female attire and confessed that he was only kidding about the name and gender thing, tried to make amends by following his father into the business of selling. He married a woman very much like his mother and raised a family of three children, all of whom were average, except for the one who was gay.

No member of the family is known to have ever seen the Grand Canyon.

Fox Hollow

Mountain Magic

A very long time ago, someone with imagination and a little daring in his soul opened an outdoor dining venue a little north of Grand Rapids called Silver Jack Wanigan. It didn't last long, unfortunately, because of inclement weather, but it was a truly unique place. Located, they claimed, on the site of an old logging camp, it consisted of an open-sided cook house, a bunch of picnic tables, and a performance area with the pond and millrace for a background. The food, slopped onto a big tin plate, was cheap, plentiful, and good. When dinner was done, we were served cherry cobbler for dessert and the entertainment would begin. We couldn't know, the one night we were there, that something else would begin that would change our lives.

The entertainment that perfect evening was a trio of musicians – mother, father, and daughter – known as the Beers Family Singers. Their rare and beautiful songs, their haunting harmonies, and the fascinating stories of their family history and the origin of their music simply captivated us. When it was over and people were shuffling to their cars in the twilight, we decided to stand in the line of people who were taking the time to chat with the singers. It took awhile and we nearly bailed out, but we felt

2,000 happy people at Fox Hollow

so drawn to them we couldn't leave. We were the last to reach them and, although we were there to express our pleasure at what they'd done for us, we felt a strong urge for something more. We wanted to *know* them. So, on an impulse, we told them of the cider-making party we were having at our house on the following Saturday and invited them to drop in. They did and it was the beginning of a friendship that would last for many years.

Bob and Evelyne Beers and their daughter, Martha, were for a time a phenomenon in the folk music business. Under contract to Columbia's Red Seal label, they toured the world as musical ambassadors for the State Department. Never rising to the Peter, Paul, and Mary level, their record albums, on several labels, nevertheless sold well and they sang to packed houses wherever they went. They appeared on my morning television show whenever their tours brought them through West Michigan and, best of all, they were our houseguests each time.

The summer we met them, they told us of their dream of creating their own folk festival. They'd moved from their home in Montana to New York State to be closer to their Manhattan talent agent. They'd bought a nearly two hundred-acre farm near Petersburg in the Taconic Range of the Berkshire Mountains with a beautiful manor house purported to have once been owned by the racketeer, Legs Diamond. It had a natural amphitheater in the forest that would be the perfect place for performances.

Thus was born the Fox Hollow Festival of the Folk Arts, to which their legion of friends and followers and other devotees of traditional music came like lemmings each August. Four days of shape-note singing, workshops, folk dancing, crafts, and night time concerts that sometimes ran to seven hours. As friends, we were invited to stay on after the festival ended. When we were able to do that, we became part of the cleanup and celebration crew. There was much to celebrate because no Fox Hollow Festival was ever less than successful.

Being there – and having a television show to which I could invite them – gave us the opportunity to get to know some of the most interesting and talented folk artists in the country who were there to perform. Like Bob and Evelyne, some of them also stayed with us when they were touring through, a bonus for us and a relief from motel nights for them.

The atmosphere at Fox Hollow was something we'd never experienced before. While the principal focus was on what happened on stage or in the treasure house of handmade items, including musical instruments, available in the booths on the midway, there was no place on the grounds devoid of something going on, night and day, planned or spontaneous. Because we always traveled there by rented motorhome or travel trailer, Bob saved a shady spot for us in the camping area reserved for the performers, where music was nonstop around the campfires. So when the evening concerts were finally over (nobody wanted them to end), we just wandered around the campground, soaking in what we'd driven across Canada to enjoy – the new songs, the story-swapping, the shared love of the great American tradition.

It wasn't Woodstock. It wasn't Newport. (Neither of those places would have dared erect an eight-hole biffy and call it "Intertanglefolkenlochenwood"). I doubt there was any place in the world where two or three thousand people could congregate that was more orderly or polite. There was no conflict, no drunkenness, no upstaging. Musicians who'd finished their sets would often stay on stage to back up those who followed. That sense of selflessness infected the audience, too. Because the amphitheater was simply a hillside in the woods, everybody brought their own chairs or blankets on which to sit. None of the usual jockeying for the best spot – and most people who had folding chairs cut the legs off so as not to block the view of the people behind them.

One of Bob and Evelyne's guest peformers was the southern gospel shouter, Bessie Jones, from the Georgia Sea Islands. One night, standing offstage and taking it all in, she said quietly, "All them people and not one police." And she was right. In all the years we were there, the only law enforcement we ever saw was the deputy directing traffic on the mountain road when the evening events were over.

Good things don't always happen because they're good ideas. In the case of Fox Hollow, there was a more important element at work. Bob and Evelyne Beers were magnets. Like us, everyone wanted to be near them, not just because their music was so hauntingly beautiful. They were graceful and loving and sharing people. Every musician who performed there said it was the best folk festival in the country because of its setting in the Berkshires, the intimate connection with the rapt audience, and the guiding presence of Bob Beers.

Then, early one morning, Bob was killed in an accident on that mountain road and the grief was felt nationwide. As a memorial to his legacy, the Grand Rapids Folklore Society moved a century- old Michigan log cabin to the festival grounds to become an archive for his extensive collection of folk arts artifacts. It was a wonderfully appropriate gesture of love and respect but, alas, without Bob's powerful presence, the festival lost its center and closed within a few years. Now Evelyne is also gone and their daughter, Martha, who lives in Canada, no longer performs.

But for us and the thousands of others who sat for hours on that hillside in the mountain forest, sometimes in pouring rain, the Beers Family and Fox Hollow are alive in our hearts. Whenever we think of them, we're grateful we took the time to invite them to come make cider with us.

L'autocaravane Et Le Chariot

Mrs. Benson would be pleased, I'm sure, to imagine that something stuck from those French classes she taught way back when we first moved to Grand Rapids. I don't remember why we took them, unless it was to make us feel qualified to walk among the River City sophisticates. We didn't learn a thing, but we grew to like the Bensons, with whom we were friends for awhile.

That, of course, has nothing whatever to do with l'autocaravane et le chariot and the encounter we experienced one summer in Quebec. Nor should you imagine that we really know how to translate "the motorhome and the carriage" from English to French, the native tongue of the citizens of that great province. It just sounds right, since the encounter involved one Quebecoise shouting insults at me in French while I countered in Air Force American.

Driving back across Canada from a New England folk music weekend one lovely August long ago, we thought a little course correction through Quebec might be fun since they had a music festival of their own going on. Cruising into town, we saw plenty of direction signs along the route, thoughtfully placed by the provincial government for those arriving from south of the border. These might have been more helpful had they been printed in *our* language, not theirs. And I'm sure there wasn't one cautioning Ne pas conduire le 26-foot autocaravane dans le vieille ville, loosely meaning "Don't drive the 26-foot motor home in the old city, dumbhead." So I did.

If you've been to the historic portion of Quebec City, you know that it makes San Francisco look like a parking lot. The streets aren't inclined – they're quasi-vertical. And narrow. And decidedly not designed to accommodate le 26-foot autocaravane. But in I drove, confident that our American derring-do would get us out again without starting another border war. And it might have, had I not turned onto a one-way street that took an oxygen-depleting change in altitude.

Though the old rented motorhome wasn't happy, it was up to the task and we were almost to the top when I noticed that it tee-boned into a cross street that was blocked nicely by an enormous fire truck. The lights weren't flashing and no firemen were about, so I presumed they were inspecting hydrants. I tooted the horn to alert them but nobody responded.

It was obvious that they were inside, doing building inspections, where they couldn't hear the feeble horn.

So, I had no choice but to stop and try to keep the bus from rolling back down the hill with a little toe dance on the brake and accelerator pedals. That's when the border war broke out. I heard a male voice shouting in French what clearly were expletives and invectives meant to hurt my feelings and those of all Americans going back to Abraham Lincoln. I looked out the window and saw behind us a heavily-loaded horse-drawn carriage unstable enough to make the driver – and the horse – fear for their lives. The man wanted me to move the autocaravane the hell out of the way before he rolled backwards down the hill. My daughter remembers that the most intelligent thing I yelled back at him was something like, "Same to ya, Jack." I'd like to think I pronounced it "Jacques," just to fit in, but I can't be sure.

The only other thing I remember about that encounter was the firemen laughing their heads off when I turned the wrong way on the cross street and had to back up two blocks before I could turn around. I'm sure Jacques and the horse enjoyed that, too.

Hidden Treasure

Way in the back of the storeroom behind my grandfather's workshop was an object that might not have seen the light of day during my boyhood. Identified by my father only as "Grandpa's cider press," it had never been put to use during the thousand weekends we spent at "Hawk Nest," his retirement home on the lower Potomac. I imagine it had seen many an apple go through it in its time because Grandpa had a nice stand of apple and peach trees in his little orchard and he couldn't have eaten them all or found enough little old widows to give them too. Those jars of amber juice in the fruit cellar must have been the result of his earlier efforts.

Many years later, when Grandpa's generation was gone and his southern Maryland property was about to be sold, my wife and I went to harvest some of the things my grandfather's loving hands had touched. From the wreckage of his old motorboat, thrown up onto the lawn by an Atlantic hurricane, we took the brass running lights and the bronze manufacturer's plate from the one-lung engine (in time, we would realize it had been built in Coldwater, Michigan, my wife's birthplace). And, almost as an afterthought, we wrestled the old cider press out of the shed and into the back of the wagon for the long ride home.

Oft times, practical gadgets emerge by necessity from activities (think the printing press and publishing or the Royce family's wheeled mop bucket). Conversely, the restoration of Grandpa's cider press gave birth to an event that became a Matthews family tradition – the Cider Squeezin' – which happened every September for many

Thelma at the crank, Buck feeding the hopper, friend Jerry Benton supervising

years. On a given fall day, as many as fifty friends would show up with baskets or bags of ripe apples and an empty jug or two. First order of business was to make cider, dropping the apples one and two at a time into the hopper while someone kept the shredder turning (and everyone big enough to reach the crank handle got a turn). Once the heavy oaken strainer basket was filled with pulp, a large wooden pressing disk would be placed atop the apples and a threaded rod would be turned slowly to compress the mash, forcing the delicious juice to flow through the slats of the basket, off the lip of the three-sided collection tray, and through a piece of cheese cloth into a waiting bucket. From there, the juice was poured into the antique keg that also made the trip from Maryland to Michigan.

Other stuff went on during the cider-making time. Horseshoes, cut-throat croquet, badminton, and just lazing about sipping cider from the keg. When the last apple had been juiced, the mob assembled in the three stalls of our barn-style garage (a gift of the '67 tornado) for a pot-luck feast worthy of the effort expended at the crank. Then, supper over, everybody assembled in the party room in the loft where the real fun began – the annual Cider Squeezin' Ceilidh (pronounced kay-lee), a Celtic tradition in which those present sat in a circle and each person in turn sang a song (or led one), told a story or a joke, played the old upright piano, read a poem, or designated someone else in the circle to take his turn. This went on for hours – and for years, as the children of our friends grew up and brought their children to make cider with Grandpa's old press.

Like all good things, the Squeezin' tradition ended when we moved to a place with no room big enough for the Ceilidh. The press, no longer useful, became a decorative piece on the deck, grew rusty (as did we), its oak frame rotted from exposure. After awhile, it became a pile of parts in the back of the garage, stabbing me with guilt every time I stumbled over it. Finally, I had to make a decision – junk it or restore it. There seemed little point in rebuilding it because we'd never use it again, nor was there anyone left in our family who could use it. On the other hand, to simply throw away all that family history went against every atom in my body.

History won out and over a period of several months, with the help of a neighbor who built a new oak frame and a machinist friend who got the rusted parts working again, Grandpa's cider press was restored to its original glory. Best of all, it's now owned by a family that reveres it as we did, both for its historic significance and for the heavenly nectar that once again pours out of the old oaken basket.

Grandpa would be pleased.

Grandpa's Pin Dish

The story that follows, "Catch the High Tide," is not a fictional work. All of the characters were real people and the setting, Hawk Nest Cottage in Chigger City, Maryland, was our family's Kennebunkport. I was the boy in the story and my grandfather, Lewis James Matthews, was the gentle soul who always had time for me and his other grandchildren. As the story notes, in demeanor and personality, Grandpa was a quiet, dignified man. He also had a keen interest in and understanding of history.

He was born in Northampton County, Virginia, in 1857, at a time when significant age difference was not regarded as an impediment to success-ful marriages in Chesapeake country. My grandmother, Anna, was only 13 when she married my 29-year-old grandfather. Sadly, Anna died at age 25, following the birth of their fifth child. Without remarrying, Grandpa kept his family together and raised the children himself. He made his living as a cabi-netmaker and home builder in Washington, DC. My father, the second youngest of his children, worked with him before going off to war with the Rainbow Division in 1917.

**Wooden pin dish
made from
David Burnes's cottage**

Washington, D.C.

*Gift of Charles O. Matthews, Jr.,
Charles O. Matthews III, Kimberley A. Van Dusen,
Judith L. Underhill, Richard Cunningham,
in memoriam, Lewis James Matthews,
2013*

As with most men in the trade, Grandpa was some-times employed to tear down old buildings. In 1894, he played a role in the demoli-tion of an historic cottage on property that was once owned by David Burns, the last holdout when President George Washington was seek-ing land on which to build the nation's new capital city in 1790. The President traveled from Mount Vernon to Davy Burns' cottage many times to

Smithsonian exhibit

negotiate with him before he finally agreed to sell 600 acres of his large plantation, on which today sit the White House and much of the seat of government.

At the time of its demolition, the Davy Burns Cottage had stood for 146 years, the oldest structure in the District of Columbia and the only building remaining from the development stage of the city. Aware of the historic importance of the little house, Grandpa salvaged a piece of rafter from the rubble and fashioned from it a small concave block of wood. Though the "pin dish," as we all called it, sat on his dresser for the rest of his life, its history was not known by my generation until I turned it over one day and discovered handwritten details of its origin put there by him more than a hundred years ago.

Grandpa's pin dish is now in the collection of the Political History Division of the Smithsonian's National Museum of American History in Washington, a mere half-mile from where the Burns cottage was built in 1748. Our family is greatly pleased that for a period of 18 months, this little block of wood was included in an exhibit of significant artifacts from the nation's formative years. Prominently displayed above it was the name, Lewis James Matthews.

Catch the High Tide

A Childhood Memory

It's like an old snapshot you might find tucked between the back pages of some long-unopened book, the details pretty much intact but the colors faded to shades of sepia. Now and then the scene reappears in my memory, tugging at me like a child not wanting to go home from the carnival, reminding me that where I'm going may not be as important as where I've been.

That mental snapshot is of my paternal grandfather opening the high picket gates of his lower Potomac home, to which we fled on summer weekends as if the British were burning the White House again. No matter when we arrived, there he'd be, opening the gates. His timing wasn't good – it was perfect. Every time.

The two-hour drive from Washington, through the red pine forests and deep green tobacco fields of southern Maryland, always ended the same way. Pop would ease up on the gas, allowing the Chevy's momentum to carry us off the Cobb Island Pike into the little cluster of saltbox cottages everybody called Chigger City, making the turn at Wilmer Johnson's house into the lane to Grandpa's place – and, sure enough, he'd be swinging open the first gate. Pop would goose the gas just enough to make it up

the lane and through the gate beneath the wooden arch and its weathered words, HAWK NEST. Grandpa, wearing his nearly hidden smile, would nod to us as we drifted through.

All of this just about sent the various women in our tribe into spasms each time it happened. They couldn't figure out how he did it and you could always count on the din in the car rising considerably at least a hundred yards before we hit the gate. One among them once suggested that the old man had finally had the stroke she'd been predicting for years and in his confusion, he just kept opening and closing the gate all day. I didn't know how he did it, either, but from the satisfied look on Pop's face, I figured *he* did. It didn't matter to me. Since Grandpa knew all that needed to be known about most everything, that little trick seemed a natural extension of his nearly miraculous powers. Years later, I sat on his favorite stump at the edge of the orchard and smiled at how clearly traffic on the Pike could be seen and heard.

My grandfather was not an ordinary man. He might have failed the Norman Rockwell All-American Grandfather Test, had there been one. He did not look like a beardless Santa Claus. He was…spare, I guess. Everything about him was in control. No loud laughter, no big talk about how great life was when he was young. His body was thin but just right for him. He was strong, even at 82, and he gave no quarter to those proudly accumulated years. The day the long-wire antenna for his old Zenith blinking-eye radio blew out of the massive oak tree beside the tool shed, he took it right back up to the 75-foot level where it belonged.

For the sake of the women, who were clustered at the kitchen window telling each other why he shouldn't be up in that tree at his age, he waited until he got back down to the 12-foot level, near the top of the ladder, before he fell out. Very conservative. But they nearly beat him to death dusting him off.

He was not one to laze about. There was a hammock across a corner of the big screened front porch – but I never saw him in it. He said it was for tourists. From that porch at night, we could see the lights from Marshall Hall, Virginia, eight miles away across the wide Potomac, and hear the dance bands when the wind was right. We'd sit out there and tear the hide off of old songs and wonder if they could hear *us*. Grandpa would rock a bit, his presence known by the glow from his pipe, but he never sang. He didn't join in the general baloney, either, content to listen for awhile and enjoy our company before turning in earlier than even the youngest among us.

His quiet contentment was misinterpreted by the women in the family, mostly his daughters, Laura and Helen, as feebleness. Never mind the 138 feet of oak tree he'd taken in stride. They placed a higher value on the 12 feet he'd skipped. They were convinced that if he didn't kill himself, he'd starve to death from his poor eating habits. Of course, they never failed to enjoy the breakfasts of scrapple and scrambled eggs and homemade biscuits he had waiting for whatever assortment of weekenders that clattered down the stairs of the old cottage on Saturday mornings. We ate those feasts – as we did all meals when the weather was right – around a long, oil-cloth-covered table on the screened back porch, facing the orchard. It was there, one glorious early fall morning, that the women made their move.

"Papa," Aunt Laura opened, "they're saying it's going to be awful down here this winter. Bad snowstorms and bitterly cold. Mike and I would love to have you come to Washington and spend the winter with us." Another old song.

He didn't look up, busy as he was fishing the last lump of his own strawberry preserves out of a Mason jar. "Who says that, Daughter?" He called Aunt Laura and Aunt Helen both "Daughter." Even when they were both present.

"A man from the Naval Observatory. Mike knows him from the lodge." Aunt Laura looked quickly at my mother and at Aunt Helen, believing she had appealed to his sense of order and logic. The other geese at the table bobbed in admiration of the man from the Naval Observatory.

Hawk Nest Cottage

Usually, he left such thrusts unparried – but not this time. "It's a well-known fact, Daughter, that people who work at the Naval Observatory rarely take note of the weather," the old man said. "Too busy looking *down*."

That one sailed right past the women, to whom it was further proof of advancing senility, but I thought Pop would drown in his coffee. I blurted a one-syllable laugh before I caught myself, realizing that I'd just seen history made. Grandpa never did jokes and that respectable little play on words made me realize that this oft-repeated assault on his privacy had caused him to call up the reserves. He smeared the delicious red lump around on the thick biscuit in his skeletal old hand. It seemed to me the odds were decidedly against the invaders. As he chewed, he gave the oak tree a glance.

"Charlie, you're no help!" Aunt Helen fired at my father. "You know he's too old to be staying in this Godforsaken place through the winter and you ought to be doing something to get him out of here and back to town where we can keep an eye on him!"

My father, like his own, was slow to anger. They were alike in many ways. Both compact, both surgically-skilled cabinetmakers, both good fishermen, and both amused at the amount of energy wasted by people intent on running the lives of other people. He looked at Grandpa as he answered.

"Girls, how'd you like to walk back to Washington tomorrow?" The morning air was suddenly very cool. He picked up his coffee cup and touched his father's shoulder as he passed. He went to the front porch to chain-smoke and promise himself that he would not be a party to such treachery.

Grandpa looked up. The blue-eyed twinkle was gone. I had to look away from what I knew was a situation already out of control. I wished myself away from there but I couldn't move. It was he who did, folding his napkin and laying it beside his plate. He took a breath to speak and I heard his teeth click as he bit off the words, "Thank you," and left the table. I heard him in the kitchen, opening and closing the icebox door – then he was gone.

There was silence at the table as they waited to hear where he was going. Aunt Helen was obviously staggered by the enormity of her gaffe, ashamed that she had hurt her father and fearful that her thoughtless remark might make him do something foolish. I saw her look at the oak tree.

When they were certain he was out of earshot, the scheming resumed, apparently already beyond the speculative stage. I felt ashamed even to be present and I couldn't listen. I moved as invisibly as I could. It was impossible not to notice, as I passed Grandpa's place at the head of the table, that the half-eaten biscuit on his plate – and the jar from which he'd salvaged the preserves – contained ants. Since there were none on the table, I knew they were in the jar when he'd slathered his biscuit. I reached over quickly and snared the plate and the jar and scraped the awful evidence into the kitchen garbage pail.

He was not on the front porch. I slumped down next to Pop. "Why are they doing this to Grandpa?" I asked.

"Oh, they have the feeling that he'd be safer and happier with the family through the winter, that's all. It must get pretty lonely down here when we're not coming down on weekends. They love him, you know. Aunt Helen didn't mean that the way it sounded."

"I know, Pop. I could tell she felt awful. But I thought Grandpa was gonna cry. He looked pretty bad when he got up from the table. Did you know he eats jelly with ants in it?"

"Yes, I know, Bo." He put his arm across my shoulder. "The old man's eyes aren't so good anymore. He probably thinks they're seeds – and they can't hurt him. It would hurt more to have one of us point out that he was eating them."

"Do you know where he is, Pop?"

"He's on the wharf. I think he's deciding whether to knuckle under or not." I was stunned. I hadn't thought there was any decision to be made. "Would he do that? Pop, you're not gonna let them take him away from Hawk Nest, are you?"

I ran off the porch, banging the screen door behind me, not hearing his answer. I hoped it would be "no," but I couldn't be certain. And I was unprepared to deal with this new and older grandfather, who fell out of trees and ate ants and couldn't be trusted to live alone anymore.

The old man was on the wharf, his back against the boat house wall, one foot on the lovers' bench, his eyes searching the horizon – for ships, or for answers?

"Hi, Grandpa," I almost whispered, feeling he wouldn't want me around under the circumstances. I was terrified of what I might see in his eyes.

They were clear and blue and confident again and my relief was immeasurable. I knew then he'd made up his mind and that the Daughters were up against something they couldn't handle on their own.

"Hi, Bud. You wanta take a trip this morning?" He held up the sack of goodies he'd rummaged out of the icebox after his breakfast exit – things he'd put together for this purpose early that morning.

God was back in His Heaven and all was again right with my world. "Yessir, I sure do. I don't much like the company back there today."

I was afraid I'd overstepped my privilege with that, but the old man smiled as he threw the cork and canvas life preservers into the flat-bottomed rowboat he and I had privately christened the *Thelma/Catherine*, after my mother and sister, the summer she was launched.

"Where we goin', Grandpa? England? Germany?"

"No, Bud. Today it's China!" He laid the big oars across the gun'ls as I untied the bowline and brought her alongside the wharf. "And today, you're the oarsman and I'm the captain."

That little exchange might have been misinterpreted by the women as an admission of old age, but not by me. To be the captain, one had only to sit in the stern, enjoying the view and acting as lookout for channel buoys, flotsam, and tropical icebergs. To row was to be in control of the course (with advice from the captain), to run the race of life and return with honest fatigue as reward. Allowing me to be the oarsman was the highest honor Grandpa could pay me – a statement that he trusted me to handle the big boat as we embarked, provisions for the long voyage wrapped in wax paper under the bow seat, for *China*!

He'd taught me well how to handle a boat – how to row in a straight line by sighting from the center of the fantail to a mark onshore or a boat at anchor or a cloud on the horizon. "You wanta tell the city kid from real people, watch how many times he looks over his shoulder to see where he's going. Doesn't help him, anyhow. He just keeps rowing in a circle 'til he rams himself and sinks." That with a wink of a blue eye.

We moved out over the green water of the tidal inlet on which his property fronted, past the little point of land that separated it from Neal Sound. Far to port, south along the Sound, Cobb Island Bridge lay bright in the morning sun, its thousand white-washed pilings and braces the landmark we called, "Germany." Ahead and slightly to starboard stood the tall black cylinder, its light blinking uselessly in the daylight, marking the tricky passage through the sandbar separating the Sound from the Potomac. This was the north end of the island, where the condition of the bottom was subject to the attitude of the river, which was known to change its mind abruptly.

"Take 'er through the channel, then cut upriver, Bud. My map shows mysterious China north of us aways."

Such voyages were not daily occurrences for my grandfather and me. Sometimes we just walked down the lane from the big gate, stopping here and there to pass the time of day with little old widows grateful for the sight of a healthy old man and a temporarily clean little boy. We'd often pause to watch the slow and loving work of Wilmer Johnson, the local boat builder, as he transformed a pile of rough cut lumber into another maritime masterpiece. His boats, always built without power tools or plans, were the most trusted on the river.

The turnaround point on our walks was almost always Cap'n Cullison's store, a shacky little structure that grew like fungus on the curve of the Cobb Island Pike. There, amidst the jumble of feed sacks and fireworks and beer bottles and soup cans and coils of new rope, sat a small display case with a diagonal crack in its curved glass front. Inside lay open boxes of Baby Ruths and Nestle's Wafers and Penny Guess Whats.

"Guess we'd better have one of those for the walk home, right?"

"Yes, Grandpa, you're right about that."

"George, two Guess Whats, please." He'd fork over the two pennies and we'd walk out into the sun again, like two barristers unwrapping their morning cigars.

"There! Off to starboard. See it?"

"What, Grandpa?"

"CHINA!"

I looked over my left shoulder, across the starboard bow and saw, lying dead in the marsh grass about fifty yards away, the huge carcass of what had once been a lifeboat from a coastal steamer.

"You're right! She's a junk run aground. Are we gonna board her?"

"Maybe not, Bud. Might be renegades below. No sense stirring up something we can't handle."

"Grandpa," I scolded him gently. "Do you really think there's something we can't handle?"

We didn't board her, of course, for there was hardly anything left except keel, ribs, and a metal hatch cover. But she was the center ring of a nautical circus to which we were admitted without tickets. I brought the boat about and backed in through the grass to lay alongside. I shipped the oars while Grandpa dug out our provisions and we hunkered down to watch and whisper and eat as the show – and the day – went on.

Small underwater sandstorms blew up in the shallow tidal pool as hard crabs scrambled for new hiding places, their eyestalks threatening us with further scrambling if we didn't lay off. One of them tried to dig a hole in a sleeping flounder and their mutual surprise was spectacular. Satisfied that we would cause no more such disturbances, teams of waterbugs resumed their Olympic games on the still surface of the pond. In the deeper water near the derelict, a sea nettle wasted its deadly waltz on creatures with no appreciation of her art form. We were startled by a whisper of movement in the darkness beneath the hatch cover and the sudden, silent appearance of a cottonmouth, so close he could have taken us if we'd interested him at all.

"That's enough for me," Grandpa said quietly. "Let's head for America."

It was only then that I felt the sunburn on my neck and realized that we'd been there a little longer than was wise. "Aye-aye, Captain," I said. "All hands on deck. Cast off the lines fore and aft. All ahead one third." I dropped the oars into the locks and took us out.

I noticed immediately that the water was both deeper and rougher, the surface textured with whitecaps. A puff of breeze pulled the used wax paper out from under the stern seat and carried it high out over the water. I never saw it come down. I pulled for all I was worth, but it was impossible for me to make headway parallel to the beach.

Grandpa's voice was reassuring as he said, "Take her out to deeper water, Bud. She'll do your bidding there. And put on your life preserver." I looked for signs of concern on his face but found none. I went for deeper water.

He was right, of course. Once out, we made good time. There was still enough city kid in me to make me sneak a peek behind me now and then to check our progress. I could see the north end of the island growing larger.

"Better bend to port now so we don't overshoot the channel in this wind!" He had to shout now. The rising wind had reached storm level, as had the sea, except there was no storm. The waning afternoon sun was still fully in command of the sky and what clouds there were had hightailed it for the horizon. It was what often happens with the passing of a cold front – but if the old man knew that, he was not in any position to explain it to me. It wouldn't have helped. I knew we were clearly in danger of not getting back to America.

I feathered the port oar and gave all my little body had in reserve to haul the starboard oar enough to turn her across the wind. She wouldn't answer to me. I looked again over my shoulder and quickly took note of what was happening to us. I didn't like it – and I was beginning to dislike all of it retroactively, including China and the water circus.

 A week or two earlier, Grandpa had taken me to "England" for a picnic. We had then also rowed out through the channel, but had turned south to go ashore on the Potomac side of Cobb Island. The wide beach and tall pines atop the high sand cliff had given us enough on which to fantasize a trip across the English Channel. The river was so quiet that day we could hear laughter from the deck of a passing steamer more than a mile out.

Now, my greatest fear was that we might be headed for England again – only this time the captain and the oarsman and the stout little vessel would be lost in the surf thundering along the island shore. I forgot myself and dropped the port oar, standing to pull harder and deeper – and less effectively – on the starboard oar.

"SIT DOWN!" Grandpa had never yelled at me before. The combination of wind and waves and threatening surf, and the surprisingly big voice above it all, did me in.

I slumped on the seat and cried out to him, "Oh, Grandpa, I can't do it!"

He got up then, cautiously, holding the gun'ls as he had taught me to do, and moved to the seat beside me. He put his arm around my shoulder and said, "That's all right, Bud. I don't think I could, either. But we can do it together, right?"

He had caught the port oar when I let go of it, keeping it from jumping overboard. He dropped it back into the lock and shouted, "PULL!" – and we pulled.

I yelled, "PULL!" – and we pulled.

We took her back upriver toward China again, a feeble old man and an exhausted, frightened little boy, straining beyond our capacity to do so, fighting for our lives, each oblivious to the frailties of the other, both more certain with every stroke that we could, indeed, do anything together.

"When we're far enough upriver to make our turn," he yelled, "we'll go straight for the beach! We've caught the high tide now, so even if we go in north of the channel, we can ride the surf through the grass!"

The mere suggestion that he had a plan for getting us over the bar gave me added strength. When we made our turn for shore and laid into it, we missed the channel by fifty feet or more – but we came in over those grass flats like we were pulling water skiers. And then, as suddenly as if a door had closed, we were in calm water again.

"Tell you what," he said to me as we were stashing the gear in the boat house, "I won't say anything to the ladies about this if you don't."

"That's fine with me, Grandpa. They probably wouldn't believe it, anyway." We hugged as we walked up the oyster shell path to the cottage.

The subject of his wintering over did not come up again. The next morning, as we hovered in that sweet half-sleep, anticipating the thump of the icebox door and the sizzle and clatter of the stovetop, we heard him fall. We found him on the living room linoleum in his pajamas. He was on his way to the bathroom, so the grownups lugged him in there and sat him on the toilet. I was appointed to keep him from falling off while everybody else flew off in all directions to find a phone or a doctor.

There was no way to tell what was wrong. He wasn't visibly ill or injured, but neither was he visibly conscious, though he managed to stay in a sitting position without much help. He was obviously making the best of a bad situation, maintaining his respectability through it all.

At some undetectable instant in that eternity of embarrassment, Grandpa settled the argument about winters in Washington. When the family arrived with help sometime later, they found me sitting on the edge of the old claw-footed tub, my grandfather in my arms.

Some have said to me since that it must have been a terrible experience for a little boy. They'll never know how grateful I am to have been with him when he died.

It seemed to me then – and still does – that we just went over the bar again.

Pop

It's pretty late in life to wonder if my children were shortchanged with me for their father. I was hardly the ever-present presence every child deserves, in part because of how I made a living. There were weeks when they saw more of me on TV than they did at the table. They were lucky to have a mother who *was* a constant presence. That they turned out well is on her, not me.

I regret this more now because I've lately been reflecting on how fortunate I was to have a father who did his job better than I have. He was the center of my life. My mother and my sister, whom I loved unsparingly, shared my life – but Pop was the path I meant to follow.

My father was a carpenter and builder (really, a cabinetmaker – a difference very much more important in the days of doing beautiful things with wood and hand tools). He was a craftsman, who never allowed a corner to be less than square or a flush trim to be anything but flush. The job was never finished until the job was *finished*. He learned that from *his* father and it was to be his gift to me. Whatever it is, do the job right or don't do it. Advice too often ignored.

Earlier than most kids get to go to the office with their dads and play with the pencils and the scratch pads, Pop was taking me to the lumberyard where he worked on Saturdays and teaching me reverence for machines. "Never turn it on unless you *know* it's not going to get you," was one of the first lessons I learned. And when he was satisfied that I understood that, he'd take the customer's purchase order, select the right piece of clear, straight lumber, adjust the saw and the stop, and lay the piece on the saw table. Then he'd look at me, just tall enough to see over the shapers and lathes and router tables, and say, "Okay, Bo, turn 'er on." And on I'd turn 'er.

Even now, many decades later, I remember the power that resulted from so simple an act as flicking a switch, feel the cool wind generated by the 16th-inch thickness of the saw blade, hear the singing of the blade as it cut cleanly through the lumber. In time, when he knew that I knew this was dangerous work and not play, he allowed me to receive the cut lumber as it came off the saw table. I learned more just watching him there and on jobsites and in the shop at home than any number of DIY lectures and Home Depot demonstrations could have taught me.

We had time together. He saw to that. We fished, dropping our double-hooked hand lines over the side of the big flat-bottomed rowboat and sitting, without talking, just feeling each other's presence. He taught me to clean what I caught, trusting me even as a little boy to gut and scale without cutting off my fingers. He was patient. He never raised his voice to me, even though I was always a work in progress. I learned from him that in Solitaire, it's better to take from the card piles on the right – and I learned what honor is from just observing his unfailing honesty. He never cheated at cards and if he discovered he'd gotten too much change, he'd take it back.

Even with all that, I didn't learn enough. I never had the chance to work with him. Much too young, that wonderfully active, funny man was taken from us by lung cancer, a souvenir he brought back with him from the War to End All Wars. I was 14 the night they wheeled away his wasted body at the Mt. Alto VA hospital in Washington. He was only 54.

I was the only job he didn't finish.

Sailing

The City of Washington, some goofball argues, was built on seven hills, portending the same fate as Rome and other fallen governments. Granted, what goes on there – or doesn't go on – adds a little color to his theory, but his topographical stretch doesn't cut it. The city was actually built on a swamp with a few modest dry land rises that we natives like to think of as hills.

Only two have any real claim to heightened consideration. One, of course, is the source of his discontent – the one all Americans know as Capitol Hill, where the seat of government has come to resemble seat-of-the-pants government.

But this isn't about that.

The other one is enough like a real hill that people used to have to shift gears to get to the top. Thomas Jefferson claimed that the earth's prime meridian ran directly through the White House and straight north up the 16th Street slope, so it came to be called Meridian Hill. And the top of

that hill figured mightily in my boyhood because a wealthy woman who lived in a castle – yes, a castle – across the street had convinced the government to buy the land in 1910 and transform it into what's been described as "an outstanding example of neoclassical park design." Some have gone so far as to compare it to a massive Italian villa, with its great tree-lined grassy mall at the top, its statuary, and its huge twelve-step cascade of water falling down the hill to the great terrace below.

Welcome to Meridian Hill Park.

One of the features of the park is the huge artificial pond on that lower terrace, too shallow to drown in but big enough for little boys and their dads to sail their pond boats for hours on end when I was a little guy. My Dad used to take me there on Sunday mornings before church to watch the beautiful model sloops and ketches and skipjacks slice from wall to wall across the clear water. I loved it and I yearned to have my own pond boat someday.

One Sunday morning, we sat on the wall next to an older gentleman with whom my Dad had struck up an acquaintance. A designer and builder of exquisite custom models, he was that day sailing a boat with a gleaming red and white hull, varnished deck, mast and spars, and bright white sails. A kindly man, he showed me how to set the rudder and adjust the sails so it would catch the breeze. A kid could not have been happier.

Well, actually, he could. When the boat completed its long trip around the pond and came back to where we were sitting, the man carefully lifted it out of the water, toweled the hull dry, and placed it in my arms. He said, "This is yours. Your Dad had me build it for you."

That boat made many Sunday voyages on the pond at Meridian Hill Park, even after those two wonderful, caring men were no longer there to share the joy with me. Today, eight decades later, it's the first thing that catches your eye when you walk into our living room, still in gleamingly beautiful condition, sitting atop the china cabinet.

With my crew, Polly and Patsy Pierson

...Two If By Sea

Before Pearl Harbor drew the United States into the war, there was a lot of reflecting by our defense gurus on Paul Revere's famous cry. Between two mighty oceans, as we were, it was unlikely the bad guys would trigger the "One if by land" alarm. If Germany was coming after us, it would most likely be a naval attack against our most important Atlantic seaboard harbors.

The government's response to this possibility was a massive project to beef up coastal defenses by reactivating and rearming the old harbor fortifications or building new ones from Maine to Florida. One of the country's most important ports of entry was Boston, a likely target. So the Defense Department created the Boston Harbor Defense Command and set about building new coastal artillery batteries on islands to the south and north of the harbor. That project was to involve our family and provide one of my most interesting and exciting boyhood adventures.

Hundreds of workers were brought in to build these installations and my father, who was at the time a civilian carpenter with the Army Corps of Engineers, was one of them. He and my mother and I, then 12 years old, (my sister, already working, stayed behind) moved from our home in Washington, DC, early in 1941 to the little village of Nantasket, Massachusetts, where the first unit was to be built on Little Hog Island.

Gun emplacement, never used

It was pure culture shock – for us and for the natives. Though many of the workers were New Englanders, most of them were from other states, the majority of them from the south. We couldn't understand the locals and they couldn't *stand* us, never mind communicating. Those people were descendants of the Pilgrims who'd settled those little seacoast villages three hundred years before, and they were about as territorial as you can get. It's easy now to imagine how they must have felt when that horde descended on them like Martians and seemed to take over their towns, filling their schools, and crowding their churches. Acceptance was slow in coming.

At Hog Island, Pop and his colleagues constructed an entire fort, armed with two 12-inch cannons capable of dropping a shell on anything afloat 16 miles out. They did this in a matter of months, finishing shortly after December of 1941, when the war became a reality and their task took on new meaning. Then we all moved on to an even bigger project on Nahant Island, where the guns were monster 16-inchers. Firing a projectile as big as a trash can, they could sink a battleship 22 miles at sea. This particular installation was on the historic Henry Cabot Lodge estate with all of the support structures – command and control rooms, ammunition storage, personnel quarters – buried underground, the guns protruding from abutments in the cliff side.

While Pop and his guys labored on Big Nahant, we occupied a rental house on Little Nahant, and though it and its companion island were both connected to the mainland by a causeway, it was a lot like living at sea. The house, situated on a cliff overlooking the ocean, was often battered by the famous Nor'easter storms. The tidal pools at the base of the cliff were wonderful places to explore at low tide. And all too frequently, my pals and I would discover bits of debris, even life jackets, washed ashore from ships that had been sunk by enemy subs far out to sea. That, and the requirement to cover our windows at night and paint the upper half of car headlights to protect our ships from being silhouetted against shore lights, made the war very real to us. Because paint was in short supply, my father blacked out his headlights with paint he made by dissolving broken pieces of phonograph records in rubbing alcohol. It didn't stick to glass very well, though, so our record collection all but disappeared.

We outlanders did acclimate to New England life and, in time, were welcomed by the residents. Because many of the workers were there without their families, my mother and father invited several of them to board with us and I remember wonderful times around the table with our extended family of five or six funny guys who were like uncles to me. And

Underground fortification, now a marine biology lab

it was while we were there on Little Nahant that I had an experience any boy would die for. Just before the project was completed, my father took me on a highly unauthorized (but likely sanctioned) visit inside the compound and down into the installation. I'll never forget the thrill of walking through the concrete ammo rooms, plotting room, and tunnels leading to the gun emplacements. It was an experience I would talk about a great deal when we were back home in Washington.

There is an interesting but sad ending to this story. Back in Washington, my father died of lung cancer (from smoking and the battlefield gas of World War I) without knowing that the big guns in these coastal fortifications were never fired. Although their subs did prowl the waters off the Atlantic seaboard and sink some ships, the Germans never sailed into Boston Harbor. After the war, the guns were dismantled and hauled away, the installations were decommissioned and many of them shuttered for good. The battery on Big Nahant served for a few years as a defense missile site, then was sold to Northeastern University for its Marine Biology program.

In 1983, when I left WOOD-TV, I had the opportunity to attend the famous Bread Loaf Writers Conference in Vermont, where I was encouraged to continue writing. On my way home, I drove down to Little Nahant to revive the memories of that interesting time in my life. On an impulse, I called the director of the marine biology lab and told him my story about the origin of his place of business. He invited me to come over and explore the place again. It was a weird, Rip Van Winkle sort of experience. What had been to me as a boy immense and mysterious and awe-inspiring – and brand new – was now much smaller, dank and dark. The concrete walls of the underground structure were wet from condensation, the overhead tracks intended to carry the ordnance to the gun positions were moss-covered and rusty. In very real ways both the place and I were victims of the forty-one years since that magical day when I'd been there with my Dad.

I thought about that period in our country's history while driving back to Michigan and was grateful to have lived it in such a unique way. Going back to Nahant was important to me and I'm glad I did it. But now and then I think that even though you can go back again, maybe there are times when it's better not to.

Breaking News!

Martians Landing in New Jersey!

Talk about your Halloween pranks – that Orson Welles, he sure knew how to pull a fast one on everybody. There we all were on Sunday evening, October 30, 1938, sitting around listening to Edgar Bergen and Charlie McCarthy and Mortimer Snerd on the radio and laughing our fool heads off. Actually, we were *watching* the radio – it's what we did, as if we stared hard enough, we could see the people on the air in the little dial window.

A good day it had been – church in the morning, fried chicken, mashed potatoes, and cream gravy for dinner – and we were relaxed, ignoring the fact that work and school resumed the following day. We lived in the stately old Chastleton Apartment Hotel on 16th Street in Washington, DC, at the time – apartment 711 – my mother and father, maternal grandmother, my sister, and me. It's how we – and most of the nation – spent our Sunday evenings, listening to Jack Benny or Burns and Allen or Eddie Cantor, avoiding the brief updates on the war in Europe.

Not everybody did that. The more intellectual among us might choose to listen to the *Mercury Theatre of the Air* on the Columbia Radio Network, where Orson Welles would present a drama featuring several actors standing around a microphone, reading their parts from scripts. Nowhere near as entertaining as hearing the repartee between Jack Benny and his chauffeur, Rochester. But on that particular Sunday night, Orson Welles did something that very nearly caused the fall of democracy. Based on a novel by H. G. Wells, published forty years earlier, the program did a dramatization of "The War of the Worlds," and did it so convincingly that word spread quickly that we were listening to the wrong programs that night.

As one by one, the nation turned to the Columbia stations, we heard news reports announcing very convincingly that Martians were invading the earth and had chosen to land in New Jersey. That, of course, should have been the tip-off that it wasn't real. From all we knew of Martians, they had better sense than to want New Jersey. Maryland we could understand, but not New Jersey. But it sounded real enough that people were rushing out of their houses as if the street was a safer place to be than their homes during an intergalactic invasion.

We could hear people hurrying in the 7th floor hallway, headed for the elevators, but we stayed where we were and hoped for the best. By doing so, we were among those who heard the end of the show and the announcement that it was a fiction. It took awhile to get the word to those in the streets that all was well and they could safely return to their apartments.

A couple of things came of all that. Suddenly Orson Welles was a force to be reckoned with and his career ascended dramatically. And we all came to realize that the radio was a lot more than an entertainment device. What we couldn't know was that it would become the cradle of my career.

Good Life

City Boy in the Summertime

Privilege comes in many forms and, in our minds, is almost always associated with money and position. Yet, even though my family was bona fide working class and only slightly above the level of poverty a good deal of the time, I think I was a privileged child.

Poor as we were, we had a maid, as almost every white family in Washington did, even when Pop was out of work and we subsisted on pots of corn meal mush (a wonderfully versatile food that could be eaten for breakfast like Cream of Wheat or potato pancakes, or for supper like mashed potatoes). The warm and loving woman who helped my mother with household chores and cared for my sister and me when Mom was busy – even when we couldn't pay her – was our Aunt Mary. She was certainly never treated as the domestics were in the film, "The Help," because we loved her more than we did some of our relatives. I was too young then to know what a privilege that was.

Unlike too many children today (like our own) who grow up in families so scattered that their parents are the only relatives at hand, my sister and I were surrounded by aunts, uncles, and cousins on both sides of the family. We also had a paternal grandfather and a maternal grandmother and a number of almost-relatives, adults who'd been close friends of the family for so long we couldn't distinguish them from the real thing. We never wanted for affection or correction, as needed. We didn't know *that* was a privilege.

We lived in a small rental house when I was a toddler, then moved to a downtown Washington apartment when I was five years old. My father, mother, sister, me, and our grandmother – too many in a two-bedroom apartment, but my grandmother shared her income from her government job and we were happy together. Apartment life was hardly a privilege for a growing boy, yet I was, indeed, a privileged child. That's because our extended family provided wonderful alternatives to life in Washington's notorious summertime heat and humidity.

I'm ashamed to say that I don't remember how my sister, who was seven years older, spent her summers but I'm sure I got the best of it. My mother came from Maryland farm stock and we had relatives who were making a meager living on their Montgomery County dairy farm. Family being family, they allowed my parents to park me with them for the summer, perhaps hoping that another pair of hands (albeit attached to a city boy) just might prove useful. I can't be sure I really was, but I gave it my best – and it was far better than summer camp (which we couldn't have afforded anyway). I was so grateful to be there in the rolling countryside northwest of Washington, I did anything they'd let me do, and maybe some things they wished I hadn't.

I learned to milk cows, getting up at five in the morning to stagger out to the milking parlor to milk the Guernsey that didn't seem to mind my unpracticed hands. For the afternoon milking, I was trusted to bring them in from the field with the help of "Shep," the family collie/shepherd, who knew more about everything than I did. I rode the stone boat, picking stones out of the plowed fields behind the two-mule team. When the potatoes were ready, my cousins and I picked them up as the toothed harrow turned them out of the ground. We thinned corn by hand, a back-breaking all-day job reducing each hill to three stalks. When threshing season came and Uncle Wilton's neighbors came in to help, I rode the wagons bringing in the wheat, then happily devoured the feast the ladies served at long tables in the yard. On rainy days, when there was nothing to do, I napped with the barn cats atop the feed sacks beneath the tin roof of the shed. And when the carnival was in town, my older cousins would let me tag along and play the midway games.

When I became a teenager, my grocery store and theater usher jobs made these summer idylls a lovely memory, but there were still times when school was out when I could spend time at my favorite place, my grandfather's retirement cottage on the lower Potomac, the place we called "Hawk Nest." There was no work there, just the freedom to be on the water, fishing or crabbing or swimming or just going where the old flat-bottomed rowboat would take me.

Contentment is an inadequate word to describe the feeling those magical times gave me. Whenever I came back to the city and compared notes with my pals, some of whose parents were in Congress or the diplomatic service and could afford air conditioning and big cars and trips to exotic places, I knew which of us was really privileged.

Your Tax Dollars at Work

There is much you don't know about your government and the people who run it. This isn't about the clown show on Capitol Hill or the not-so-Secret Service or the Department of Homeland Insecurity. It's about the regular stuff that keeps the wheels of Democracy turning.

I'm qualified to comment on this because I'm a member of that increasingly endangered species, native Washingtonians - one of the six or seven still living who were born and raised there. I fished and swam in the Potomac. The President occasionally attended my church. There may be buildings still standing there that were built by my grandfather. My father helped build the old Washington National Airport (now Reagan). My parents are buried at Arlington Cemetery. And in my youth, I worked for the Federal Government. So, I know something you don't know.

What I know – and I'm not sure you want to know – is that in the summertime, the Government of the United States is run by teenagers. No joke. I know this because during the summers when I was in high school, I wasn't a car wash attendant or an ice cream scooper or a grocery stock boy (I did that during the winter). I was – and many of my friends were – employed by the Federal Government to replace fulltime employees who were on extended vacations.

I spent two summers at the Treasury Department, one at the Pentagon, and another at an agency I no longer remember. You will not be pleased to learn how those summers went. The first year at the Treasury Department, I was assigned to participate in the redemption of World War I Liberty Bonds, which had finally matured. There were about ten of us in a large room that was furnished with six or eight 16-foot-long tables and a number of rolling swivel chairs. The tables held huge old-fashioned ledger books bearing the serial numbers of all the Liberty Bonds sold during the war. Each day, a very large bin would be rolled in, filled with packets of bonds. Each bond bore a serial number. Our job was to find the ledger containing that number and stamp the date next to the number. Pretty simple on the face of it – except the numbers in each packet were random, requiring us to move from table to table and ledger to ledger in search of the corresponding numbers. Being kids, we discovered that the rolling chairs made it possible to rocket around the room, like bumper cars, in search of the numbers. We got so good at it that we'd have the entire bin emptied before lunchtime. And nobody got hurt.

I don't recall much about the second time I was at Treasury, but I don't have any trouble remembering something that happened on my way to work one morning. I wasn't a kid who could afford a car, so I bicycled, my paper lunch bag clutched in my left hand, my right hand on the handlebar. Downtown Washington traffic wasn't what it is now, but it still had its hazards. One morning, as I was freewheeling along, a car pulled up several yards ahead of me and about eight feet from the curb – plenty of room for me to zip past. Had I known the driver was dropping someone off, I wouldn't have zipped. This dawned on me at about the time I reached his back bumper and the front passenger door opened. Too late to unzip, the bike and I and my lunch bag wound up in the front seat of the car with the astonished passenger and driver, who were amazingly gracious and forgiving. The only lasting damage was the embarrassment I still feel. And I've always wondered if they've told this story as often as I have.

I remember just three things about my summer working for the Department of the Army at the Pentagon. The lunches at the kiosk in the big park-like inner courtyard were to die for. My very pleasant supervisor's name was Mr. Smelly. He wasn't. And there was a locked drawer in one of the file cabinets marked "Atom Bomb." Nobody ever opened that drawer while I was there.

The real eye-opener was the summer desk job at the unremembered agency. In the Federal Government in those days, everything that moved from office to office traveled with a little blue, numbered routing slip attached. As each memo or piece of mail reached its destination, the slip would be initialed by the recipient and sent to a clerk for filing in numerical order. I presumed the system was in place so that at the end of the day, they'd know if something was missing. I was subbing for the clerk whose duty that was, and I was very conscientious about doing a good job. I kept those little rascals neatly stacked and secured with rubber bands so they wouldn't get mixed up. Oddly, I wasn't required to list the missing slips. Each day, just before five, a courier would load them in a wire basket and wheel them away. Curious about my role in the working of government, one day I followed the courier to see where he was taking my little blue slips. It's worth noting that the person for whom I was filling in was a career Civil Service employee probably pulling down twenty-five grand a year (good money back then). Ready for this? The little blue numbered routing slips *went to the incinerator.*

Is this a great country or what?

Galilee

A Week That Was

Growing up in the Nation's Capital gave me lots of experiences to remember. Standing along Pennsylvania Avenue as the President – FDR – rode by in the big open Packard; marching as a High School Cadet in inaugural parades; listening to the National Symphony Orchestra from a canoe by the floating stage at Lincoln Memorial; watching houses afloat on the flooded Potomac; attending sunrise services at Arlington National Cemetery with my church youth group.

In fact, some of my most memorable experiences are ones I shared with my rowdy Methodist Youth Fellowship gang. Chief among them was a week we spent each summer in the mountains of western Maryland with other MYF groups. Pleasant Valley Camp was a cluster of log cabins and a central lodge in a pinewood forest above a perfect glacial lake. A week in a place like that never failed to tame the wildest among us. I'll never forget the last time I was there.

At breakfast the first morning, we noticed a stranger in the dining hall. Bearded, quiet, and oblivious to the youthful clamor in the place, he seemed not to be a part of it all. We thought he was a camp staffer or a group adviser, but he wasn't. Throughout the week, he was always alone, contemplative, apart from the softball games, singalongs, prayer circles, and general collective foolishness. We couldn't figure him out, so we stopped trying.

There was always sadness on the last full day of camp, knowing that the new friendships we'd made might not last beyond our bus trips home. Because of that, the closing event on Saturday night was truly meaningful to each of us. We gathered around a bonfire on the beach, told ghost stories, talked about what the week had meant to us, sang some camp songs and hymns and were led in a brief, spirit-filled ritual called a Galilean Service. Galilean – as in Galilee.

It always ended with the group leader lighting a candle from the fire, then using it to light a cup candle each of us held. After the last note died out, we would put our little candle boats in the lake and walk back up the hill in reverent silence. I remember that when we reached our cabins, we turned to watch our candles spreading out across the darkened waters.

But this year was different. While we were singing our last hymn, the worship leader did not light his candle but, instead, went out to the end of the dock and waited. We then noticed a rowboat coming around a bend in the lake. As it drew closer, we could see a figure standing in the prow of the boat. A robed figure holding a burning candle. A *bearded*, robed figure. And thus was the mystery solved. We knew who he was and why he was there and it was very cool.

As the man rowing the boat feathered the oars to keep from bumping the dock, the bearded one, looking eerily like the Jesus in the painting that hangs in every Sunday School room, made the classic mistake of someone who knows little of boats. Holding his candle out toward the man standing on the dock, he leaned out and placed his other hand on the edge of the dock. The boat, of course, immediately shot backwards, leaving the counterfeit Christ slung like a hammock above the water, his toes hooked over the edge of the boat, a one-handed death-grip on the dock, the free hand still bravely holding the candle aloft.

What happened next makes walking on water seem like a carnival trick. The toes and the hand lost their purchase on boat and dock simultaneously and the bearded, robed one simply sank out of sight - except for the hand with the candle, sticking out of the water like a submerged Statue of Liberty. The vesper leader, not wanting to waste their careful staging, did what anyone would do in such a situation. He knelt down and lit his candle from the one sticking out of the water, just before it sank out of sight. Getting to his feet, he came back and lit our candles, said a little prayer (speaking loudly in a vain attempt to cover the background sounds of splashing and gasping), then each of us walked to the edge of the water and launched our little candle boats.

Perhaps the most astonishing part of the whole evening was the fact that a bunch of normally exuberant teenagers, having just witnessed what amounted to a bad vaudeville act, left the beach as silent as monks and made it all the way back up the path and into our cabins before we all fell down laughing.

Today, 70 years later, a handful of old people, living in various parts of the country, share one indelible, youthful memory – the sight of a soaked and shivering figure huddled in the prow of a rowboat, disappearing around the bend of the lake, followed by 50 little floating candles.

We're still laughing.

Faith
...and Hope

There is a question I will never ask another person because whenever I've been asked, "Are you saved?" I've resented it. It's one of those "When did you stop beating your wife?" questions for which there is no answer that doesn't incriminate you. If being "saved" involves some thunder and lightning moment, the truthful answer invites what I consider to be an invasion of spiritual privacy. And this late in life, I might never experience that glorious moment because I'm still busy working it out.

Among the people I most envy are those who possess unquestioning faith. To know without question that God is alive, Jesus is in the Garden, and St. Peter is at the gate must make life a lot like standing in line at Dairy Queen. You're just a place away from reaching your reward.

I don't mean to be flip about this, because in no way do I take it lightly. In very significant ways, it is the theme of my life that I lack what others seem to have in abundance – absolute faith. Several years ago, our pastor asked a few of us in the congregation to speak about our faith and how it affects our lives. When I was asked to participate, I came close to declining because I knew I couldn't fake it – not in church. I had to be honest. It wasn't easy looking into the faces of the certain, talking about my uncertainty

Let's get something straight. I'm a card-carrying, life-long member of the Methodist church and I'm devoted to its message of inclusion (though the argument about gays in the clergy seems to be the highlight of every Annual Conference). Like its founder, John Wesley, it believes in community service. Without its open Communion table and tolerance of pastel Christians like me, I'd have no place to take my fragile faith for improvement.

When I was young, my faith was new, and clear, and positive. I believed then what I was told – and I knew that those who were guiding me truly believed what they were telling me. But my weakness has always been my analytical approach to everything. I could never be satisfied with anything without first knowing how and why – and inevitably it revealed how many things in life, like much of the Old Testament and the nonsense that God likes us best, can't be explained. Anything that isn't logical is hard for me to accept as fact, therefore.......well, you know the rest.

And, lately, the amazing, frightening discoveries of the realities of the universe simply scare the daylights out of me and leave me to ask, again, how could one Mind, however great, conceive of and control all of that and still keep His eye on the sparrow? Yet, considering the important role church membership has played in my life, the narrow escapes I've had, and the many times my prayers have been answered, my questioning borders on rank ingratitude. I *want* to believe. Unlike those who are satisfied in their unbelief, I want it all to be true.

So, if you're looking for me on a Sunday morning, you'll find me in the fourth row at Marne United Methodist Church, opening my mind and my heart to the possibilities. There's room for you, too.

The Face on Page 287

From the *Grand Rapids PRESS*, May 2, 1982
(Written for a special section featuring first-love reminiscences)

Getting away from home wasn't so hard. I was ready to leave. My family had no tradition of sending men to college and there was no precedent for seeing the oldest son (in our case, the only son) desert the historic trade. We'd all been carpenters, back to where the footprints disappeared in the dust, yet no one thought I should do anything else but go to college. Our legacy was the craft, not the family business (there was none), and the time had come for someone to learn to do something else – if that's what I wanted to do.

Getting me into college was the problem. The ones I'd selected as good prospects weren't much interested in me. That's when I learned how important it could have been to pay attention and study in high school. My Sunday School superintendent got me into college on the assumption I was bright enough to take advantage of the chance to be somebody. It wasn't difficult for him to arrange; after all, he'd just been appointed president of the school. Were they going to tell him no? It's too bad they didn't. Somewhere out there in the world, somebody's trying to make it without a college education because I took the last place in the Ohio Wesleyan class of '52.

I was clearly not ready for what I was to encounter in the exotic city of Delaware, Ohio. College was like Friday night at the movies! It was magical. The Old School. Freshman beanies - English muffins for breakfast (I'd never seen one) – hot roast beef sandwiches for supper – all-night bull sessions – sweetheart serenades, panty raids, and pep rallies. The air seemed always filled with the sounds of glee clubs, marching bands, and the skittering leaves of those breathless autumn football Saturdays, when we all yelled, "Rowdy-Dow!" and the Battling Bishops beat the enemy senseless at old Selby Field.

How could I not fall in love in such a place? We were the children of destiny, arriving in the nick of time – even ahead of Gene and Roy – to save the dying world. Romance was unavoidable. It was the year Cleveland won the Series and Dewey lost the election. Bonnie Prince Charlie was born in Buckingham Palace and poor Kathy Fiscus died in a well. Five thousand airplanes flew into Berlin and five thousand alumni blew into

Delaware to cheer for the Red and Black at Homecoming. And I lost my heart to Emily Richards.

There's no memorable story to our meeting. I just looked up one day and there she was – shorter, smarter, and more sophisticated than I, and older by two semesters. A computer trying to match us would have died in the attempt. I was brash and funny, naïve, immature, rudderless, and undisciplined. She was quiet, modest, classy, and somewhat mysterious. Her dignity and her sense of values made me better than I was. My wackiness made her happier than she'd been. Like flowers in the shade, we grew toward each other's light.

We made no promises. It was too risky. I walked with other girls sometimes. She danced with other boys. It hurt in ways we dared not talk about, so we stopped doing that. We skirted the future with cautious conversations couched in wouldn't-it-be-neat-ifs and yeah-that-would-be-greats – and I could have died from the pain the night she told me she was in love with someone smart and wonderful, destined to do great things – and it was *me*!

Becoming a better person, however, did not make me a better student, and Ohio Wesleyan wisely gave up on me after my sophomore year. In danger of giving up on myself and needing to make a gesture, I chose to go to war. After basic training and tech school and just before my squadron sailed for Korea, I went to Connecticut to meet Emily's family and engage in serious negotiations for the future. They would find me older and wiser – and careful enough to have the money for the ring rolled tightly in a pair of socks in the bottom of my duffle bag. The visit would be shorter than I'd planned.

Emily met me at the bus station, driving a powder blue Cadillac convertible. A nice touch, I thought, but unexpected. It was the first of a series of surprises I would suffer in quick succession. The next two were the second and third Cadillacs in the driveway of their summer home in Fairfield.

We had never discussed her means at school. There wasn't any reason to, although my student loan and hardship scholarship were no secret. It was a strange experience to discover that the sweet and simple girl who'd shared those afternoon drives along the Olentangy in my disintegrating Model A was an heiress.

Not until late that night, after a very formal and polite candle-lit dinner with her mother and father and younger sister, was I able to be alone with her and breathe again. I held her and found courage I'd not had back at school. Gone were the what-ifs. I said what I felt and told her about the money in the sock. The social differences fell away and we talked about the future and laughed about the Cadillacs. When we kissed goodnight at the guest-room door, I was closer to Heaven than Methodism had ever carried me.

Over lunch at The Club the next day, I waited for my chance to declare my intentions to her powerful attorney father, who was delivering a stirring summation on the joys of raising children, giving them the good things of life, and seeing them turn out to be what you've hoped they might be: wise and discriminating. It was man to man, with a fatherly flavor – a message that began to sink in about the third time he introduced me to one of his barrister chums as "one of Emily's young friends from college." Suddenly, sitting there in my baggy khakis amidst all that linen and mahogany and sharkskin, I knew I could never justify my futureless presence in his daughter's life. I did not ask for his blessings.

Later in the day, in Em's absence, her mother took me aside and put my worst fears into words. Surely, I wanted the best for Emily if I loved her as I said I did. Certainly, I was too fine a young man to ask Em to wait until I determined my course in life. Perhaps if we waited until my Air Force enlistment was up and I was on track again....

I walked to the bus station in the dark without saying goodbye. It was, I thought, appropriately dramatic for the monstrous agony I felt. How could something so good be so wrong? How could I have been dumb enough to think I could live up to Em's expectations? Emily herself answered the questions, squealing to a stop beside me in her father's limousine and jumping out to embrace me. What was the idea, running out like that? Her mother didn't run her life, she told me. She could make her own decisions. Yes, she loved me, and yes, she would marry me if I still wanted her when I came home.

Although our correspondence failed to compensate for the long separation, we managed to bridge the 10,000-mile gap with words of love and hope. We observed each other's accomplishments but carefully ignored the subtle changes in ourselves. When I came home a staff sergeant, much more a man but no less a child, she was no longer a college girl reaching for identity. By then, she was a research assistant making it on her own, freed from her dependence on family wealth and surrounded by new friends.

We spent important times together walking in the New England woods, grateful for having known and loved each other and promising never to forget how much it had meant to us. Her mother had been right after all. I wasn't ready for marriage and wouldn't be until nine years later.

Em lives now somewhere in New York state with her husband, their three children having graduated from college. I think of her once in awhile and hope life has been as good to her as it has to me. Her face shines out from page 287 of our old year book, and I wonder whether she ever looks at the boy on page 258 – and smiles.

The face on page 258

The Great
Uniontown Bus Incident

Like everyone, I have often been the victim – and the beneficiary – of circumstances. So often, in fact, that my dreams are sometimes like a movie loop that just keeps playing back weird episodes and events. It's like repertory theater – the same characters playing different roles in different plays, the titles of which are "The Fake Jesus," "The Bees in the Wood-chips," "Folk Music in the Berkshires," and that all-time favorite, "Driving the Bus in Uniontown."

Some of these stories – all of them true - long ago became part of my spoken repertoire, told on the air or in dinner speeches or, more often than my family cares for, in the company of friends. I can't help myself. It's the kind of stuff that never seems to happen to other people and it's too good not to share.

The bus in Uniontown is a good example. Following my sophomore year at Ohio Wesleyan, I followed my fraternity brother, Herb Detweiler, home to Uniontown, Pennsylvania. His father, who was the local Studebaker dealer (anybody remember those?), had offered me a summer job as a car washer and errand boy at the garage. It was a nice gig – not a lot of brainpower needed –summer in the mountains with room and board provided in the big, noisy Detweiler household, hanging around cars, driving customers home, moving cars around the lot, flirting with the secretaries. That, and plenty of time alone in the wash bay to make plans for saving the world.

And then came the bus incident. Behind the dealership was a big city parking lot, which the company was also allowed to use for overflow parking. Unlike the slick, automated ramps and lots of today, this one was unpaved and had an old derelict city bus used as a toll booth. One day the service manager tracked me down and said he needed my help with something. The city had decided to pave the lot and put in parking meters and asked the dealership to move the bus to a park on the other side of town, where it would be left for kids to play in. Not exactly kid friendly by today's standards, but we didn't worry about kids that much back then.

The game plan was for the service manager to tow the bus with the company's big highway wrecker and my job was to simply steer the old behemoth as it followed the wrecker. Sounded like fun to me, but I was too young to understand the possibilities with which the whole project was fraught. While the service manager hooked thirty feet of chain to the front of the bus, I got into the driver's seat and pretended to know what I was doing. I just took it for granted that the service manager knew what *he* was doing.

He started the truck and eased forward until the chain was taut, spinning a little gravel against the front of the bus, which was understandably reluctant to give up the position in which it had been sitting for 20 years or more. Our little caravan slowly circled the lot to line up with the entrance and eased down the alleyway toward the cross street we would travel to the park. When the truck reached the street, the coast was clear, so the service manager turned right and I prepared to follow him, straining against the very stiff mechanical steering. It was then that everything went very wrong. Driven by a man who'd obviously forgotten his geometry, the wrecker was already going east while the bus and I and most of the chain were still in the alley going south.

What happened next is the part of the incident that still occasionally comes back to disturb my sleep. At the corner of the alley and the cross street, there was a little one-story, one-room shoe repair shop. There is reason to use the past tense in referring to the little shop because with no horn and no brakes, I couldn't let the service manager know that he was dragging the bus sideways right through that little building. By the time the wrecker was yanked to a halt and the service manager looked back, it was too late. The bus and the building had become one and I was cowering in terror as a little Italian woman was beating on the side of the bus and screaming at me in language her mother surely hadn't taught her. And although I was innocent of the crime, I just wanted to figure out how to open the emergency door and escape, find my car, and get the hell out of Uniontown before Father Detweiler got hold of me.

Although a story like this is best left without a conclusion, it's important to recall the miraculous forces that came together to make things right without my losing my life. As it happened, Mr. D. was out of state at an automobile dealers' convention and Herb's oldest brother was running the business in his absence. He somehow managed to bring together the insurance people, the lawyers, a contractor, and the shop owners, who conspired to erase the awful evidence before the boss got back to town.

A few weeks later, summer was over, Herb was back in college, and I was in Air Force basic training in Texas. And although he and I and our wives have remained friends for more than sixty years, I've never been back to Uniontown, Pennsylvania.

Candy
A Shameful Admission

The trouble with letting your friends know you're writing a book like this one is their insistence on the inclusion of every cockamamie story you've ever told them. Why they'd want to *read* what they've already *heard* too many times (do you hear my wife's voice?) I don't know, but what the heck. Their memories are apparently more forgiving than mine, so here's another of those who-else-do-you-know-who'd-do-something-like-that stories that have tinted (not tainted) my life.

The problem was that I didn't smoke. I'd pretended to in high school but never inhaled. When I got to college, believing that real men smoked pipes, I bought a cheapie and a bag of something called Evinrude (the outboard motor people?), stoked up, and promptly burned a hole in my sweater because I couldn't keep the pipe in my teeth. So much for smoking.

Whatever else you might say about the American military, they fed us well and did their best to cater to our tastes, such as hot coffee, cigarettes, and candy. Those of us lucky enough to be where we could eat in mess tents, never wanted for sufficient nutritious food, piled generously on our tin trays by the mess sergeants and orderlies as we moved along the chow line. And at the end of the supper line was a guy who dropped a pack of cigarettes and a candy bar on our trays.

Well, of course, I'd given up smoking before I died of embarrassment, so I always traded my smokes to one of my tent mates for his candy bar. Made us both happier warriors. Then along came Lent and, as I had been taught to do by my Methodist forebears, I had to deny myself something for those 40 days. I decided to give up candy. That is, I decided to give up *eating* candy for 40 days. So, every night during Lent, I threw my two candy bars into an AWOL bag under my cot and suffered the proper sense of denial.

Then along came Easter and under my cot was a bag with 80 candy bars in it. Now, it's worth noting that the Air Force did not try to stick us with those desert ration type candy bars made of chocolate that wouldn't melt in a blast furnace. Those babies were full-size Mounds and Baby Ruths and Three Musketeers and York Peppermint Patties, made with the most delicious chocolate available in the free world. And there, beneath my cot in that penetrating Korean springtime heat, was a bag containing 80 uneaten candy bars.

When I dragged the bag out and dropped it on my cot to gaze upon my spoils, the contents didn't feel at all like 80 individually-wrapped objects but more like a sack full of pumpkin innards. It might have been easier to drink them with a straw than it was to peel them and lick the contents off the wrappers. But I was a trained killer, equal to whatever my country demanded of me, well-taught not to waste anything. In deference to starving orphans through the world, I ate them all in one week.

Sorry, God.

Bob and Me

Ten Days on Bread Loaf Mountain

In the summer of 1983, when TV8 discovered it could survive without me and I was invited not to come back from vacation, I was okay with it. I hadn't been happy for awhile. I'd long since been replaced on the weather broadcasts by someone who actually knew what he was talking about, my show had been off the air for more than a year, and I wasn't enjoying the stuff they had me doing. After 21 years on the job, I was surplus goods and I knew it. I also knew I'd been lucky to last that long in a business as fickle as broadcasting. It was time to move on.

There, however, was the rub. Move on to what? I only had two marketable skills – talking and writing. I had a few free lunches with people who thought my visibility might make me useful in their businesses, but none of them interested me. I had four offers to go into Amway but I didn't think I'd do well knocking on doors, carrying a suitcase full of face cream. So I just went to the cottage and fished and did some writing and waited for lightning to strike. When Labor Day came and the summer people split for home, I was alone at the lake and lightning had not struck. I had some free-lance work but no steady employment.

There were blessings, to be sure. I was well and I had a wife who really understood how incomplete I felt. "Maybe this is the time to concentrate on your writing," she said. "Why don't you see if you can get into Bread Loaf?"

I'd heard about the Bread Loaf Writers Conference a few years before from a journalist friend in Traverse City, who'd been there.

Photo by Ed Brown, courtesy Middlebury College

The Inn on Bread Loaf Mountain

Located on Bread Loaf Mountain in an ancient resort hotel near Grafton, Vermont, the conference is a division of Middlebury College. The oldest and most prestigious of all such operations (Robert Frost was one of its founders), it is a very tough nut to crack. In order to be permitted to even apply for attendance, a writer must submit a sample of a contemporary work – which places you in a pool of fifteen hundred hopefuls. If the work shows promise, then you may apply and hope the committee thinks you're worthy to walk among the two hundred fifty writers accepted each term. I had no chance, but a wife who insists without nagging is a rare and wondrous thing. I sent them my one short story.

My attitude then was pretty much in line with my feelings all those years earlier when I'd put my hurriedly-written patriotic essay on Miss Whitford's desk. And this time, I wasn't just up against kids from schools across the city of Washington, my stuff would be compared with entries from across the country and beyond. Nice try. Then the letter came.

Robert Frost's cabin

The ten days I spent there on the mountain in the company of those widely talented, creative people, some in their teens, some middle-aged, a few in their last years, was one of the most inspiring experiences of my life. The place itself was a delight. A very large, three-story inn was the centerpiece. Nearby was an old theater building once used for shows put on by traveling entertainers, now the conference lecture hall. Spread out along the meadow road were other old tourist buildings, now used for housing for conferees. And a monstrous barn, now the social center of the conference grounds.

Every day was packed with seminars, lectures, one-on-one advisory sessions with published authors, shared reading of our works, late-night bull sessions in front of the fireplace in the cavernous barn, and, often, just solitary walks on the wooded paths on the mountainside.

Robert Frost's own log cabin writing retreat was just a mile down the road and I hiked down there some early mornings when the dew made my pant legs wet. For a writer (or someone who thinks he's one), standing on ground once walked by a man so revered in the craft is an intensely personal thing. Unsure of my talent as I was, I could almost feel his hand on my shoulder, wordlessly urging me to believe in myself and to keep writing.

That was more than thirty years ago and the spirit of Bread Loaf is still very much with me. I'm no more sure of my talent now than I was when I imagined old Bob's encouraging touch there on the steps of his little cabin. Maybe the difference is that now I understand how forgiving readers can be. Someone once told me that if getting up and speaking in front of groups of people made me nervous, I should remember that not one person in the room would want to change places with me. Maybe that's it. Readers are glad someone else is writing stuff they can read.

I sure hope so.

Unfair!

An Uninvited Opinion

There is a lot in life that I know little or nothing about. Many of the things that make the world go 'round, stuff we take for granted, are just mysteries to me. It's fair to wonder how I made a living knowing as little as I do about most things.

One such is the fine art of picketing, which, in my view is a colossal waste of time and energy. With apologies to all the overworked, underpaid people who spend days shuffling back and forth in front of plant gates carrying signs calling the company and management bad names, I don't get the sense of it at all. First of all, the suits have already heard the bad names across the table, so the signs mean nothing to them. More often than not, the bigshots avoid the pickets anyway by using their private entrances.

And if the point is to draw sympathy from the passing public, the effort is futile because most of us just feel embarrassed for the people on the picket lines and look the other way.

Picketing seems to be a lot like trick or treating. Time was when strikers made their point by getting into some serious mischief, like taking pokes at their colleagues who elected to keep working or flattening the tires of the bosses. By walking around in a circle with signs on their shoulders, pickets may hope to give the impression that they're just this side of busting out some windshields, but in this more lawful age, the implied threat has lost its edge. Most of the people on the line are about as likely to engage in violence as some nine-year-old is to knock over your privy because you shorted him on the Milky Ways.

Solidarity is a very good thing. Dignity is even better. Face it, most people have little regard for pickets, even if they know enough about the grievance to be on their side. And workers who've served their employers faithfully and with distinction hardly gain the respect of their bosses by looking silly and useless on the sidewalk. Maybe there are rules I don't know about, but it seems to me that unions could serve their members better if they didn't require them to just walk around during a walkout.

A better strategy, one that would raise awareness of the value of these temporarily idle people, might be to have them apply their energy toward the community good – volunteering at daycare centers and homeless shelters, repairing homes for the elderly, or just cleaning the streets around the plant. They might still be able to get their message across by wearing bright shirts that say, "SHAME!" or "UNFAIR!" or "DON'T BUY THE CRAP THESE PEOPLE MAKE!"

Okay, maybe not that last part.

Choosing

A Game Not Unlike Marriage

For a short time early in my career, I worked the all-night shift on Detroit's WJR, keeping company with a vast and lonely band of truckers, waitresses, nurses, and just plain insomniacs spread across the country. Like other disc jockeys, I sometimes played the "Desert Island" game with the audience, asking them to send me a list of ten books and ten records they'd want to have with them if they were ever stranded somewhere for a long time.

The results were always interesting, sometimes amusing, often predictable. Now and then, I'd change the rules and suggest they pick human companions instead. In that variation, they had to choose just two, not ten. Two is much harder than ten. And neither could be a living family member.

My own participation in the game was usually limited to reading other people's choices on the air. I couldn't really settle on a list of books and records that would endure beyond their current popularity with me, knowing that I'd tire of reading and listening to the same stuff over and over. People, I figured, would be another matter. Choosing them wouldn't be any easier, of course, but I had more confidence that my interest in them would last.

A few practical thinkers suggested that a nice combination would be any one of several popular lovelies and a reliable obstetrician. Those with loftier ideals were in favor of companions who would stimulate them intellectually. The bow-tied presidential candidate Adlai Stevenson was a hot number in those days. Others opted for anyone whose knowledge of physics and nature would be useful in overcoming the dangers of exposure, coupled with a military pilot trained in survival tactics. Perhaps a good Scout leader who knew how to make fire with sticks.

Inevitably, there arose a debate over the gender of the two companions. Two men? Two women? One of each? The latter combination would likely lead to problems of jealousy, rivalry, favoritism, and, possibly, ostracism. Not a good thing for the long haul. One clever futurist among the listeners thought it best to select two women – one a registered nurse or physician, the other a botanist, and both pregnant with children of the opposite sex.

Obviously, you'd have to hope that your choices would be healthy and emotionally stable, but short of extensive physical and psychological testing, how could you tell the nuts from the bolts? And there was the possibility that no matter how able and appealing they might be when you washed ashore, you might soon wind up climbing trees just to get away from them.

I wrestled mightily with this one – the audience insisted upon it – and gradually narrowed my list down to battalion size before I threw up my hands and changed the subject. Even now I'd have a terrible time choosing among the many people who inspire and appeal to me.

My greatest fear, however, is that, given the choice, neither of them would pick me.

Deprivation

When my wife and I moved into a brand new home in a senior living community recently, we were more than ready to give up the six acres and the house in the country. In these new digs, the landlord is responsible for the care and maintenance of the place. Such things as lawn care, snow removal, and fixing what's broken are no longer on me.

I miss them.

Okay, maybe I don't miss having to shovel the walks and clean off the roof – but mowing was never work. And, frankly, I liked the challenge of figuring out what's gone wrong and dealing with it without having to pay someone else to do it. I'm just a DIY kind of guy.

But, there's more to it than no longer being responsible for keeping the place up. It has more to do with not having an excuse to stay prepared. I used to be in Menard's so often they offered to give me a cot in the basement and have my mail delivered there. I used to study their section in the Sunday paper, just to see what I needed.

I loved to hang out in thrift shops and secondhand stores and junk yards and go to farm auctions and flea markets and yard sales, just to see what's there. I never came home empty-handed. I'm a used-stuff kind of guy. But the practical one in the family reminds me often that we no longer have a basement or a garage big enough to accumulate any more stuff.

Likewise, there's no point in going to the Home and Garden Show or the Cottage and Lakeshore Living Show because we don't have a garden or a cottage anymore.

Don't get me wrong. I'm very happy with our new life, our new home, and our new neighbors (though they have a long way to go to match our old ones). We're comfortable.

There are some things I refuse to give up, however. One is the Y's Men's Club's annual White Elephant Sale. I've never missed one, and I'm not about to begin now. You just can't have too many three-ring binders, window envelopes, and sheets of foam rubber.

There's still room under the bed.

Grass

One of the few downsides of giving up the responsibilities of keeping up the homestead is the matter of grass. I always marked the end of a long, cold winter by hearing the inner alarm of my body clock telling me that mowing time was coming.

Strange, isn't it? For all its delights, I may have enjoyed warm weather simply because that's when the grass grows fastest and I got to cut it most often. My wife interpreted this as another example of the inherent madness of men – the highly overstated guy thing. I don't know. Maybe she's right. Maybe we really are from Mars. No, that can't be. There's no grass there.

It was the ritual of mowing that I loved – the ceremony of opening the shed where the gleaming green tractor awaited, checking the oil, cleaning the air filter (now and then), filling the tank, hearing the engine roar to life, backing out into the sunshine. The real joy, however, was in shifting into drive, dropping the deck, engaging the blades, and heading out to drive the familiar, two-acre rectangular pattern for two mindless hours. You just can't touch that. The fact that the grass got cut while this was going on was mere coincidence.

I know that to a man who works his heart out for a living aboard a big Allis Chalmers, Case, John Deere, Minneapolis-Moline, or Oliver, the sight of us make-believe farmers on our little toy Craftsman lawn tractors is ridiculous. Nevertheless, it made me feel good to take control of those sixteen dainty horses under the hood and skillfully maneuver around the nasturtiums and dogwoods without having my hat blow off. And when I was finished and looked back over my manicured masterpiece, I thought, "Let the neighbors top that."

It was easy to imagine a collection of onlookers as I rode to glory each time. When I finished hosing out the mower deck and drove slowly back into the shed, I'd cut the engine and swing down from the comfortable molded seat and acknowledge the imaginary admiring crowd. And I would remember something Cale Yarborough said one year after winning the Indianapolis 500: "Shucks, it wasn't anything. I just kept turning left."

More Vox Populi...

"Weathermen, weathergirls, give us a break,
Agree in your forecasts for our sanity's sake.
Terry says 'stormy' while Matt Kirkwood says 'fair.'
Craig James calls for sunshine, Peter Chan cautions care.
We shouldn't complain over divergent views
For the weather sure beats the political news.
Dave McIntyre predicts for the County of Barry.
He soothes our fears when Bill Steffen is scary.
If our favorite forecaster we had to choose,
We'd say, 'That's easy, bring back Buck Mattyoooooooos!!'"

                              Kensington Jones

Irresponsibility

Like most adults, I have a reasonably sound sense of responsibility. I choose to follow most of the rules of life simply because not to do so would require having to explain why I didn't. I don't speed anymore (and regret ever having done so). I observe ozone non-action days. I recycle. I walk facing traffic. I watch for ice on bridges. I conserve water. I clean my plate (but not when there's squash, liver, eggplant, black olives, or mushrooms on it). And I pretend not to enjoy the television commercials for Victoria's Secret.

But I freely admit to one great failing. Despite all the warnings about the consequences, I can't bring myself to floss. Over time, I've endured hours of lectures from dental professionals who like to cite me as an example of what can befall any child who fails to floss regularly.

The reasons for flossing do make good sense – even to me. It's the mechanics of the exercise that I just can't master. The denticians scoff at this, but they learned how to do it on rubber dummies with jaws as big as automobile trunks. For me, trying to get an assortment of fingers and thumbs inside my mouth in order to yank a piece of cinnamon-flavored twine back and forth between my teeth ranks right up there with installing kitchen faucets for sheer lunacy.

So, I go through life trying not to soil my cage or spoil the party, but often failing at the basics. I just hope that if I make it to the Pearly Gates, St. Peter will recognize me, even without teeth.

More Vox Populi...

"Handsome and mild-mannered,
To us he appears on TV.
A gracious smile, yet all the while
He's not what he seems to be.

With smile so bland, wave of a hand,
He'll tell you that all's fair and clear,
When at the start in his black heart
He knows the storm is near

The information he receives
Is of the very best.
He doesn't read, he doesn't heed,
He makes his own wild guess.

Violence and crime will fade
With a bit of luck.
Our problem is, it seems to me,
How to get rid of Buck."
                    An admirer

Senior. Living.

Whenever I leave my doctor's office, I feel pretty much the same as I did when the bell rang and class was over and I'd escaped again without being caught with my homework undone. The doctor-patient experience is, of course, different at 86 from what it was at 56 – or any of the other sixes after age 40. I'm always early for my appointments, perhaps because I fear they'll call roll and mark me absent. The result, of course, is that I'm put in the little room much earlier than necessary and told the "doctor will be right in." And he is. Right in the little room next door, where I can hear his muffled conversation with someone whose solitary wait must have been similar to mine. I don't blame the doctor for the wait. You learn soon enough that the appointment time is not when you should expect to see the doctor face to face. Given the variety of reasons patients come to see them, it's not reasonable or logical to expect doctors to stay on schedule. There's no equality of need between a splinter in the pinkie and a bowel obstruction.

I am a grown man. Of sound mind. I've made a decent living. I've stayed out of trouble mostly. I get along with my peers. Some people think I'm a smart fellow. But I sit in the little room awaiting the arrival of the doctor in much the same frame of mind as when I sat outside the principal's office, wondering what I might say that would convince him that my life is worth living, or, in this case, worth saving. I actually catch myself practicing how I'll respond to his opening line: "Hey, how're we doin' today?"

Clever? *"Better than you. I can walk out of here. You have to stay and keep talking to old cranks like me all day."* Serious? *"Not bad. That thing I was in here for last week seems to have gone away on its own."* Defensive? *"Get that license from Sears Roebuck?"* Compassionate? *"I won't take up much of your time....."*

While he flips through the telephone-book-sized, encyclopedic record of my infirmities, genuine and imaginary, I look for clues that will tell me how quickly I'm sliding toward the abyss. And when it's over and I've escaped again without the verdict we all know is coming, I walk out into the sunshine healthy and free, grateful that my "health care provider" hadn't seen the fear in my eyes or detected the slight pain behind my knee that had prompted me to see him in the first place.

But the miracle is that the moment he walked into the room, the slight pain behind my knee was no longer there and when I walked out into the sunshine, I actually felt better. The guy is a very good doctor.

And the co-pay was only 20 bucks.

Unintended Consequences

Nausea, rash, vomiting, diarrhea, burning sensation,
Itching, wheezing, coughing, irregular heartbeat,
Muscle weakness, bloating, seizures, lethargy,
Memory impairment, sore throat, cramping,
Bloody stools, swelling of ankles, anxiety,
Hallucinations, mental confusion, fatigue,
Chest pain, lightheadedness, heart failure,
Eye discoloration, difficulty swallowing,
Stomach pain, rapid weight gain, chills,
Erection lasting more than four hours,
Mood swings, fever, disorientation,
Outbursts of anger, loss of appetite,
Shortness of breath,
Hiccups,
Death

"Better Things for Better Living Through Chemistry"

More Vox Populi...

"No doubt you watch the weatherman
And note the weather signs.
X's mean we'll have more snow,
Rain is slanted lines.

H and L is air pressure.
It's either high or low.
Arrows mean directions
From whence the wind will blow.

And should he draw a ringlet,
Beware, my friend, BEWARE.
It means there's trouble brewing,
TORNADOES in the air.

Triangles are the symbols
Of a cold front on the way.
And if the map is free of marks,
It means a pleasant day.

If the forecast doesn't please you,
Well, folks, that's your tough luck.
He's merely a reporter –
Don't put the blame on Buck."

Author unknown

T.M.I.

Maybe

Since this is the last book I'm likely to write, this may be the last chance I'll have to talk about a matter I've been reluctant to discuss in public. Maybe it is Too Much Information, but by not revealing it over the long years I've been on the air, I've done a disservice to people who might have benefitted from knowing that I live with a condition called gran mal epilepsy. I never kept it a secret from my friends and colleagues because, for me, it's never been a big deal. It wasn't diagnosed until my early 20s and hasn't affected my career in any way.

Epilepsy is a serious condition for many people. The seizures that result from it can be frequent and debilitating. I once knew someone who had many seizures each day. Compared to people like that, I hardly qualify to carry their bags. I've had fewer than ten seizures in my life and, thanks to modern science, none in the last 40 years.

But I never talked about it on the air because I feared that people would think of me as a television announcer who had epilepsy instead of just a television announcer. In a very minor way, I'm sure it's what everyone goes through who differs at all from the general population. Neverthe-less, I regret that I didn't have the courage to speak openly about the fact that it's possible to live a perfectly normal life, even with occasional short circuits in your wiring.

And as long as we're considering my health (you'd think I was running for office), there's another little thing I've been dragging around with me. Many years ago, I was waiting at a traffic light and noticed that one of the city's nice new buses, picking up passengers across the street, had a big dent in the side. But as the bus pulled away, the dent didn't go with it. Then I noticed the light pole was crooked. I looked at other objects and found they were distorted, too. A visit to the ophthalmologist revealed that I had early onset macular degeneration, a condition that destroys your central vision, and that I would likely be legally blind within two years. The diagnosis was only half correct. Yes, I have it. No, I'm not blind. Over the years, it has become a bit more difficult to read, but I have no trouble driving or doing anything else that requires me to see what I'm up to.

In comparison to others whose bodies have been their enemies, I am one lucky dude. I've had a couple of back surgeries and some corrective work done on a knee and a shoulder, but, so far, I've been blessed with good health and the ability, as Garrison Keillor says, "to get up and do what needs to be done."

Who could ask for more?

Silver Lining

I have long held the belief that the best is yet to come. Maybe that's because it so often has. When my plans don't work out, something better usually happens. For example, the three times I've been fired from broadcasting jobs all led to opportunities I wouldn't have had if I'd stayed where I was. It's not a formula I'd recommend for career advancement, but it worked for me.

I think of myself as an optimist. Why else would I leave my porch light on when the Prize Patrol is in town? Why do I keep buying Lotto tickets, even when the jackpot is a measly two million? That's called making your own luck. But I'm not opposed to accepting help when it's offered.

You ever hear of Raylene, the Ohio psychic? I received a letter from her one day – maybe you did, too – in which she told me that beginning in January, I'd have 72 days of continuous good fortune. To guarantee this wonderfulness, she would send me an energized 14-carat gold key to hang around my neck. All she asked in return was a check for $12.95 to cover the cost of handling and postage (and, possibly, the payments on her new home in Hawaii). I thought about it but I was pretty sure the key would turn my neck green before the good fortune set in.

I had a much more personal encounter with the infamous astrologer and prophetess, Jeane (that's how she spelled it) Dixon, one morning on my television show. When she walked into the studio, she gently took my ring fingers and looked into my eyes. I thought for a minute she was going to propose. Instead, she told me that something truly wonderful would happen to me the following April. We went on to have a friendly and spirited conversation about her ability to foresee things, great and small. Among them was Russia's launch of Sputnik, the assassinations of Mahatma Ghandi, Jack and Bobby Kennedy, and Martin Luther King. I thought if this lady could pull those off, I was in for a pretty interesting April. And I wouldn't have to pay for handling and shipping.

So, when the next April came and went without any noticeable improvement in my fortunes, I checked to see what else Miss Jeane might have missed. Imagine my disappointment when I learned that she'd also predicted that Pope Benedict would be assassinated and be the last Pope,

World War III would begin in 1958, cancer would be eradicated in 1967, and world peace would come in the year 2000.

I still believe the best is yet to come. It just won't be lady psychics who make it happen.

Challenger
Written on January 28, 1986

The unthinkable has happened. The inevitable has happened. Before noon this morning, on its voyage into the great unknown, the world watched the Challenger Space Shuttle disintegrate into roiling white plumes of smoke and steam against a sky so blue as to make us think it impossible. Before our eyes, the end came, not just for the wondrous machine that goes and comes routinely now, but, more importantly, for the seven remarkable young people with the courage to ride the whirlwind that is space flight. Among them, the first (now maybe the last) Teacher in Space, Christa McAuliffe, a New Hampshire high school history teacher.

If anything could make this disaster more awful, it's the fact that her students, as well as students in school districts across the country, were watching as the shuttle lifted off, listening to the play-by-play coverage of the last moments of their teacher's life. What must they have thought? And what of the 11,000 applicants she beat out for the privilege of dying in a space suit? How must they feel now about coming in second? A little guilty, probably, for being grateful to have missed the cut. And what of the journalists, like our friend John Hockenberry, who still wait for their chance to go? Second thoughts?

The universal mourning that is setting in over these very visible deaths might seem to some a little unfair when we barely notice the more numerous victims of terrorism and hunger. It is, of course, their very visibility that is the root of it. It's because we knew them so well – as a group and as individuals. They were the new celebrities. We'd been invited into their lives. Their going took a part of us with them.

24 times we've seen that strange mechanical marvel thrown into space and wondered at its durability and preciseness. I remember our awe and pride – and patriotism – as we watched the first shuttle's homecoming. I stood with colleagues in the television control room and searched with the network cameramen for the speck emerging from the blind silence of reentry. Its appearance was more thrilling than any of those three-chute splashdowns of earlier spacemen. There it was, dropping like a skipstone on its last lift, headed for the only chance to land safely. It came on as if the craft and the crew were participating in just another routine training drop from the belly of their 747 mothership. I remember, too, that after

she rolled to a stop, the crew had to stay aboard, hatches battened, for several hours because nobody knew how fit they might be after days in space. By the time Challenger was coming in from the regular run, the crew hopped out and walked around like Pan Am pilots getting in from Pittsburgh.

The shuttle missions brought space down to earth for us. The earlier programs were beyond our grasp; much too risky for us mortals to want to be a part of. When Alan Shepard sat up there, strapped to the warhead, I had no desire to be there with him. When John Glenn disappeared over one horizon and reappeared behind us, his orbit seemed less risky than Shepard's simple ballistic shot – but still infinitely beyond me.

That first mechanical landing on the moon was a corker. I'd watched that, too, from the control room, the action appearing as a succession of black and white still shots on the screen, the rocks and sand growing larger as the nearest foot of the lander touched down. The first manned landing was again an event beyond my sense of reality.

I first became aware of the shuttle program during its development phase when a representative of the contractor, Rockwell, appeared on my television show with his white plastic models and portfolios of pictures and charts and talked confidently of the future of manned space flight which lay within reach. I liked that the vehicle looked like an airplane, not a missile. I liked the fact that the crew could get up and walk – or float – around in street clothes, instead of being imprisoned in flight suits. And I especially admired its utilitarian aspects – its enormous cargo space and big bay doors, like a sleek and graceful semi in the sky.

I'd also had a revealing conversation with Alan Shepard and realized that the astronauts were not supermen, possessed of the traits my comic book heroes displayed. Shepard was an ordinary guy who mowed his own lawn and fixed his own car. He went to work like everybody else – except when he went to work, he didn't come home for half a year.

Because of guys like him, the whole space program has been a shared experience. We've been there as the crews changed from groundlings to astronauts, playing at weightlessness, getting in shape, practicing landings. We've watched them at work in the cabin, in the cargo bay, and out there dancing on the rim of oblivion, herding home an errant satellite.

But 23 successful launches and landings gave us a false impression of perfection. When Columbia's flight two weeks ago set new records for delays in getting up – and down, a small red light went on in my gut. Where's the perfection we're used to? Then the hacksaw episode with the balky hatch yesterday and the small electrical malfunction this morning and my sense of foreboding flashed again.

Now the worst has happened. Not just a malfunction, not a fire on the pad like the one that killed Grissom, White, and Chaffee, but a spectacular explosion during launch at that point in the flight when there is no chance of survival if things go bump. And just like that, seven brave, dedicated Americans are vaporized.

So, what happens now? Well, if we're smart, what happens now is we all go back to the first square. The program goes into suspension while an investigation works to eliminate the cause of this tragedy. And then the program goes on, doing what it was intended to do, develop the means for man to travel and live in space – on other worlds, other universes. We owe it to the ten courageous people who have thus far given their lives to go where no man has gone before.

Addendum

Those thoughts came back to me in a rush 17 years later when the grand old lady of the shuttle fleet, Columbia, broke up on reentry and scattered her remains, and those of seven dedicated astronauts over most of Texas. Already in decline, the shuttle program would end in 2011, with NASA concentrating its energies on developing the hardware and the means to head for deeper space. The surviving shuttles, Atlantis, Discovery, and Endeavor became permanent displays at museums in Florida, Virginia, and California. The prototype vehicle, Enterprise, which never went into space, resides aboard an aircraft carrier in New York harbor.

And now there are well-funded commercial operators who are building new ships for what we once thought was mere fantasy, space tourism. Test flights have begun and tickets are selling. The future is here.

More Vox Populi...

"Here's an ode to little Art
Whose mother feared Buck's wind-chill chart.
Long johns, britches, gloves, and sox,
Shirts and sweaters out of a box,
Caps and mittens, scarves and boots,
Earmuiffs, leggings, oversuits.
She dressed him warm against the cold.
He staggered out as he was told.
They found him dead upon the stoop,
Standing there with little droop.
Art didn't fall when he reached the end;
He was dressed so warm he couldn't bend.
He didn't freeze as anticipated -
Little Art had suffocated."

M. P. Thrud

Mail Call

I have a special relationship with the mailbox. For me, not much beats the joy of getting mail, a condition that set in during my college and Air Force years. I recall a terrible few weeks while I was in Korea when, for no known reason, the mail plane came with nothing aboard addressed to me. When the dam finally broke, the mail clerk handed me 20 letters and two packages – but in the meantime, I'd lost ten pounds and couldn't sleep.

Conversely, when I lost my big-time Detroit radio job, I received almost 1,500 cards and letters of condolence. It was almost worth getting canned to get all that mail (I was so grateful, I answered every one that had a return address). So I welcome whatever appears in the mailbox – junk mail included. Garden catalogs, pleas for money, political rants, contest material, bills for things I didn't buy, I'm a happy dude. Stuff that's addressed to "Occupant," I regard as personal mail. After all, I am the occupant. It was in my mailbox. That's personal.

But the mail isn't quite as much fun as it used to be. Having discovered the cyber highway, a lot of the old-time con artists don't spend a lot on postage anymore. It's been a long time since I received an offer to help move inheritance money out of Nigeria. The guy who sold burial plots in Arizona doesn't write anymore. The supplier of giant Mexican wedding hammocks has taken his business elsewhere. And the New York postal clerk with the sure-fire formula for beating the horses is nowhere to be found.

Must have been something I said

Except for the ever faithful Publishers Clearing House, most of those promises of great wealth have dried up. One year, I kept a running account of all the sweepstakes offers I received. In all, there were 39 from nine different sources. And it wasn't just money they dangled. I could have won two Buicks, two Jeeps, four Fords, a Plymouth, a Mercedes, four TVs, two computers, a complete phone system, two cruises, and a dream vacation home. I entered every one of them.

But I miss the mail order guys most of all because I used to be one of them. Back when I was breaking into television and not at all sure it was a reliable way to make a living, my wife and I started a mini mail order company that sold a little garment that tied in back and looked like a vest. We purchased them from a local corset and brassiere manufacturer and advertised them as The Veste - "for the gay blade or the home bartender – a practical and attractive complement to your best suit or your favorite sport jacket (we had no shame). Red poplin with brass buttons and white felt press-on crest. Fits sizes 32 – 50. $2.00 postpaid; 3 press-on initials 25 cents extra." Stop laughing. We actually bought a one-inch ad in PLAY-BOY. The orders rolled in. A dance band in Indiana bought 12 of them. We broke even.

But wait. A few years later, when the man-on-the-moon thing captured us all, I scored an exclusive deal with a company that made inflatable moon globes. This time, we bought $700 worth of TV time, cut a commercial, and ordered enough moon balloons to float the Costa Concordia. We had it going there for awhile. A couple of libraries and a few teachers bought them but there seemed to be a limited need for inflatable moon globes. We broke even again.

My love affair with the mailbox is hardly quenched. I keep hoping I'll hear from Nigeria and I might need one of those Arizona burial plots one of these days. In the meantime, I'm waiting for the next big thing to come along. Maybe this book is it.

Big Apple

It's easy to forget, here in the polite and proper provinces, the acidity of the city. Those of us who willingly, happily live in Keokuk or Carney or Grand Rapids, with our Victorian value systems and our mutual respect, have either been spared or have forgotten the incredible, all but impossible, experience of getting somewhere in New York City.

I'm not talking about Getting Ahead, difficult as that is when competing with the largest concentration of humans on the planet. I'm talking about getting From Here to There in an environment in which everybody else is trying to do the same – and most of them are coming upstream. This also has nothing to do with driving in New York, an activity that requires only a horn and a death wish, and should not be attempted by anyone who has not already made peace with God and the family.

I've been to Chicago, Atlanta, Boston, St. Louis, Los Angeles – even Seoul and Tokyo. I grew up in the District of Columbia and spent two years in Manhattan at Columbia University. So I'm trained in the Mobile Arts. But the peaceful personality of inland America matches my own, and this slow, sweet life had dimmed in me the exhilaration of Big City walking until I had to spend a week in conferences in the "greatest city in the world" (lower case intended).

It took a couple of days for the killer sidewalk instincts I had developed in my Columbia days to return and revive the pure joy of broken field walking. I left the Hilton, across 6th Avenue from the ABC studios, at noon on a Monday with the intent of *strolling* through the theater district – just to see the marquees and the ten-story billboards and the strange little people at war with the world. Of the latter, my recollections now are like oil paintings in my head: a man wearing a rubber raincoat on a hot July day, the Lord's prayer printed endlessly in half-inch white letters on its dirty green surface; the pitiful bag ladies; the unlicensed and highly profitable sidewalk vendors, their contraband spread out before them on sheets or blankets. The strolling, however, was short-lived. I was soon aware that I had never *strolled* in New York City. I had *competed*.

Walking in midtown Manhattan is not unlike playing football, except for the absence of helmet and pads (both of which could often be helpful). The same skills are required: grace, flexibility, coordination, body control, courage, and unwavering determination to reach the goal line. My old style reemerged quickly, and I was soon following my blockers, picking my path, dodging, twisting, juking, breaking into the clear.

Compared to sitting in small groups or listening to mind-numbing tutorials, that day on the sidewalks was invigorating. I didn't like New York any more than I had when I was there before, but I could remember how good I was at coping, and how skilled I almost always was at bucking the crowds. Almost always.

There was that day, on my way to class, fast-walking the field, using the piles of garbage bags and sleeping vagrants as blockers to hit the secondary at flank speed – only to find myself suddenly suspended in mid-air over a subway entrance.

It didn't end well.

The End is Near

In a book I wrote about the history of my little village Methodist church, I went on about the fragile folks who were certain the end of the world would occur in their lifetimes. They'd been given ample opportunity to worry about it because every ten years or so, somebody comes up with a new theory on why the lights are about to go out.

Remember Y2K? A minor percentage of our fellow Americans were girding their loins, stockpiling their non-perishable food and water, oiling their weapons, counting their ammo, and digging their moats to fend off the rest of us. Although that particular cataclysm wasn't expected to be terminal, those true believers did sincerely expect all systems to stop and we'd be thrown back to living off the land – or them – and they'd clearly forgotten their lessons about sharing.

Then somebody who reads too much ancient history discovered that the big stone the Maya had used for their calendar only had room for 5,125 years. The last date thereon inscribed was December 21, 2012, so the word went forth that we should all get our affairs in order, hold hands, close our eyes, say a little prayer, and...........what? It bothered me that the all-knowing alarmists couldn't tell us what the end would be like.

And don't forget those great interpreters of the Word who confidently offered a money-back guarantee that the world would end when they said it would. The once would-be Republican candidate for President of the United States and televangelist, Pat Robertson, said the door would slam in 1982. I think he was disappointed. And remember Harold Camping, the 99-year-old lunatic millionaire California radio preacher? He and his little flock were packed and ready to go in 1994 and mocked those of us who laughed at him. When his appointed hour came and went, he picked two more dates in 2011. He finally gave up and died himself. Nobody went with him.

This stuff fascinates me. There's a philosophy that if you always expect the worst, you'll never be disappointed. But this goes beyond pessimism. How deep does your disappointment in life have to be to drum up some reason to scare the hell out of the rest of us? And this is nothing new. This doomsday forecasting has happened more than 250 times down through recorded history (and probably plenty of other times before pencils were invented).

And why was this pertinent to the history of Marne United Methodist Church you might ask? Because a Methodist preacher named George Bell and a few of his clergy pals beat Pat Robertson and Harold Camping to the punch in the 1750s, predicting that the elevators would stop running for good on February 28, 1863.

It's safe to guess that all of these doomsayers will finally be satisfied about five billion years from now when, we're told, the sun will finally run out of gas. We'll just have to wait and see.

Reunions

For reasons bearing mostly on my immediate departure from my home town after graduating from high school, I've never attended any of my Washington, DC, class reunions. Two years in college, four years in the Air Force, another year in college, employment several states away, marriage, job changes, all gave me the excuse I needed not to return to celebrate the great escape.

And *that* was part of it, too. My class had graduated without me because I wasn't serious enough to keep up with them. If it's true that Mark Twain actually said, "Don't let schooling interfere with your education," I was his man. Elsewhere in this book, I say that I wasn't stupid, I was bored. That's only partly true. I was, indeed, bored – *and* stupid. From grade school on, I had very little interest in the learning process because I already knew all I wanted to know. I wasn't gifted and I didn't have a learning disorder. The teacher who told my mother that I was a dreamer probably got it right. It's embarrassing to admit that I simply didn't pay attention in the classes that didn't interest me. In English, social studies, music, military science, and architectural drawing, I was an alert student. But math, science, foreign languages and anything else that might have been applicable to getting and holding a decent job made me cower in the back row praying not to be called upon. All of that cost me an extra year in high school and erased any desire I might have to go back and celebrate our collective triumph over education. It also made me a secretly understanding parent when my own kids occasionally faltered in school.

This came back to haunt me one recent weekend when my wife and I attended her 60th high school class reunion. It was a pleasant weekend of driving about the town she grew up in, seeing places she'd told me about, capped by an evening of conviviality among the people with whom she'd shared those places and times. In the midst of the frivolity, there was also quiet mourning for the 39 out of her class of a 121 no longer present. And it was easy to guess in watching those on hand that even more would not be back for their 65th reunion.

For me as an observer, not a participant, the joy of the event was tinged with sadness. Here was a room full of people who had once been 18-year-olds, differing in a hundred ways except for their common belief that their lives would be better than their parents, and their desire to get on with life. Now, they were their parents, a collection of old people, differing mostly in their health and their journeys, come back to their starting point, wondering where their lives had gone. It was hard not to imagine that behind some of the smiles and the handshakes and hugs was a touch of longing, a wish that they might go back to that magic moment and do life over.

I don't mean to cast a pall over their celebration, for there was much to celebrate. There were stories to tell and retell, old friendships to revive, the air filled with laughter and "remember when" and, at one poignant moment, the spontaneous raising of their collective voices in their class song, "You'll Never Walk Alone." I envied them and regretted again not having known that the time would come when I would want to convene with the people I once wanted to forget.

By their very nature, reunions are gatherings of survivors. But they're also an acknowledgement that whatever they'd done with their lives, wherever their journeys had taken them, it was necessary not to forget where they'd started and with whom they'd shared that beginning. I know that a life that doesn't come full circle is a life incomplete. That's why my ongoing friendship with a few people from high school days is important to me. Although we didn't graduate together, we share both the memories and the regrets of life passing away too soon. In small ways, our correspondence is our reunion. But it's hard to sing your class song in an email.

Knee Slappers

I'm no less prone to laughing at bad jokes than the next guy – and, like everybody else, I can't remember the good ones long enough to repeat them. Of course, the circumstances in which you hear a joke contribute mightily to your appreciation of it and your likelihood of remembering it.

The five gags that follow, I can truly say, are my favorites of all the thousands I've heard in my lifetime. If it happens that you don't find them amusing, try telling them in your own words to someone else. I guarantee you'll both laugh.

The Parrot and the Magician

A magician working a cruise ship is constantly annoyed by the captain's parrot, which observes all his illusions with a bright and mischievous eye, then announces to the audience how the trick was done. Just as the prestidigitator unveils his big finish, the ship strikes a derelict mine, blows up, and sinks. A half-hour later, the magician regains consciousness, clinging to a piece of debris, on which also rests the parrot. The parrot eyes his fellow survivor menacingly for a long time, then says, "Okay, wise guy, I give up. What'd you do with the ship?"

The Drunk and the House of Ill Repute

A young man, far removed from home and loved ones and consumed by a desire only loneliness can produce, knocks on the door of a brothel. The proprietress welcomes him but tells him that there is only one young lady idle at the moment and there are no rooms currently unoccupied. It being a warm night and his loneliness so great, he asks if he might spend his time with the young lady on the roof. In the midst of their spirited appreciation of the occasion, they roll too close to the edge and fall off. The event, though fatal, does not dislodge them from their embrace, a sight that does not escape the attention of a passing drunk. Filled with civic responsibility, he knocks on the door of the brothel. The proprietress opens the door and says, "Yes, my good man, what can I do for you?" "Nothing, ma'am," he says, "I just thought you ought to know that your sign fell down."

The Boy With the Golden Screw in His Navel

A child who was born with a golden screw in his navel suffered for years from fear and embarrassment. His parents sought to have it removed surgically but were advised by their pediatrician to leave well enough alone. The child was otherwise healthy and whole and, besides, it might be worth something some day. But the golden screw brought continual grief to the child, who was teased; then to the boy, who was laughed at; and to the young man, who was the butt of many locker room jokes. He tried everything to remove the screw himself but nothing worked. Finally, he determined to make a pact with God. "Remove the golden screw and I'll do anything you ask of me." Confident that God would grant his wish, he slept soundly through the night. When he awoke, he threw back the covers *and the screw was gone*! Overcome with joy and gratitude, he leapt out of bed – and his ass fell off.

Mrs. Smith and the Famous Faith Healer

A world-renowned faith healer had set up his tent in a new town and was having difficulty getting the spirit to move his first-night congregation. Feeling the need to show some evidence of his powers, he called for two people with special needs to come forward and allow him to prove himself. Very hesitantly, a man with no apparent physical limitations and a woman on crutches presented themselves. The preacher asked the woman her name and the affliction that troubled her. "My name is Mrs. Smith and I have a leg injury that won't heal." He asked the man the same question. With a decided lisp, the man answered, "My name is Jone*th* and I have had thi*th* li*th*p thin*th* I wa*th* a *th*mall kid." The preacher saw real promise here. "Mrs. Smith and Mr. Jones, the Lord and I can help you both. Just step behind that screen and listen to everything I have to say." After two or three minutes of impassioned prayer, the preacher said, "Mrs. Smith, throw your left crutch out here." The crutch came over the screen and clattered to the floor. "Now, Mrs. Smith, throw out your right crutch." The crutch followed the first one over the screen, accompanied by a stirring among the people in the tent. Confident that he had taken control at last, the preacher called out, "Mr. Jones, how is it with you?" Jones answered, "*Th*well, but Mi*th*ith *Th*mi*th* ju*th*t fell on her a*th*!"

Jesus on the Golf Course

On ascending into Heaven, Jesus is invited by St. Peter to see how the place has improved during the time He's been on Earth. When they reach the new nine-hole golf course that had been installed behind the new community center, the two decided to knock a few around before lunch. As the newcomer, Christ tees off first but tops the ball badly. It rolls about six feet and drops into a gopher hole. Suddenly, the gopher appears with the ball in his mouth and takes off across the fairway. He gets about ten yards and a hawk swoops down, grabs the gopher in his talons and flies off. Halfway down the fairway, an eagle dive bombs the hawk, causing him to drop the gopher. But before the little rodent hits the ground, the eagle grabs him and heads for his nest in a tree behind the club house. As he flies over the green, he's hit by a chip shot and drops the gopher, who lands so hard the ball pops out of his mouth and rolls into the cup. Back on the tee, Peter turns to Jesus and says, "Okay – are you gonna play golf or are you gonna fool around?"

Well, they were funny when I heard them.

"No, Thursday's out, Buck. How about never -- is never good for you?"

Used with permission. ©Robert Mankoff/*The New Yorker Collection*, 1993

More Vox Populi...

"Absolute knowledge I have none
But my aunt's washerwoman's sister's son
Heard a policeman on the beat
Say to a laborer on the street
That a medicine man in Borneo
Knows of a man who claims to know
A Chinese coolie in Timbuktu
Who said that the heathen in China knew
Of a college man in a southern town
Who got it straight from the circus clown
That he had a son who had a friend
Who knows when winter is going to end."

                                    Author unknown

The Million-Dollar Gamble
The Little Brown House in the Woods

Nothing Blue Lake Fine Arts Camp does should ever surprise anyone. From the moldy mattress days of its genesis in the mid-sixties to its present five-star reputation as one of the world's premier summer arts education institutions, it has always done what it thought it could do. Never mind the skeptics, never mind the pitfalls – and pratfalls- of going where angels wouldn't go. If it seemed like a good idea, the intrepid founders, Fritz and Gretchen Stansell, would just go do it, thank you very much.

Of all the amazements that have happened over the decades in this serene corner of the Manistee National Forest, few could have been more audacious and seemingly ill-advised than adding a broadcasting division to the young organization. Housing, feeding, inspiring, and teaching more than four thousand kids every summer was responsibility enough without adding the Olympian sport of jumping through regulatory hoops, raising money, and devoting the time necessary to pulling it off. Way too much for the faint of heart.

But this is Blue Lake Fine Arts Camp we're talking about here, decidedly not the faint of heart. They saw the need. There was no radio station serving this area with fine arts programming. Who better to solve that problem than a fine arts organization? Next question.

Deciding to do it was the easy part. Getting it done took up a whole chapter of Fritz Stansell's charming book, *Blue Lake Fine Arts Camp: The Early Years*. It's a painful, funny story with a cast of characters who refused to listen to those who said it couldn't – shouldn't – be done. And, like everything else Blue Lake has accomplished, defying the odds just added to the satisfaction of making it happen. It was the classic Little Engine That Could story.

Starting in 1982 with an inexperienced staff and an often-interrupted six-hour broadcast day, the skeptics (including me – and I was on the station advisory committee) weren't convinced the little engine would make to the top of the first hill. But within three years, WBLV was broadcasting around the clock to a growing, grateful, generous audience. In 1994, its sister station in Grand Rapids, WBLU, went on the air, further widening its services and its audience.

At this writing, Blue Lake Fine Arts Camp is in its 50th season. Its 1,400-acre campus contains many examples of its belief in the possible, including its new Rose Theater, an authentic replica of London's historic Globe Theater, site of performances of Shakespeare plays each summer. Its broadcast division, now operating from newly-expanded studio facilities, has been on the air for thirty-three years. The stations are serving a vast portion of western Lower Michigan, as well as a worldwide audience through the internet. It is widely regarded as one of the nation's best Public Radio stations and I'm proud to look back on the ten years I served there, first as Program Director, then as General Manager. Having spent the greater part of my career in commercial radio and television, it was fulfilling to work for an organization whose mission is bringing people to the arts.

Wonder what those rascals have up their sleeves now.

New performance studio at Blue Lake Public Radio

The Other Corner Office

When I went to work at Blue Lake Public Radio as Program Director, it didn't take long for me to discover how much I'd missed the atmosphere in a radio station. Late one night, I was sitting in the production studio, listening to audition tapes, looking for the particular voice I wanted to add to our young staff. They were all precise in their delivery, nicely modulated with no reading mistakes, clear evidence that they'd been taped over and over until they got it right. I knew this, of course, because I'd done the same thing years earlier when I was trying to land a job. Audition tapes are innocently fraudulent because everyone wants to make the best impression possible in the few minutes (seconds, often) they're being heard by the person who decides their fate. It's why I always preferred live auditions in which I could observe how an announcer would make and recover from a mistake. Poise was far more important than perfection.

WBLV was still on an abbreviated broadcast schedule, so I was alone in the building. I was getting a little bored, listening to all those earnest voices, when I became aware of a sensation I hadn't felt in a very long time. There is a pulse in the air in radio stations that is undetectable to people who've never worked in the business. It isn't audible and it isn't explainable, but there is a rhythm there – and when I felt it, I knew I'd come home. That may sound a bit romantic, but it's true. And when I became aware of it, I went back and listened to some of the tapes again because I knew I had been listening with my ears and not my heart.

The administrative staff at Blue Lake Public Radio when I got there in 1985 consisted of the General Manager, Development Director, Office Manager, and Program Director – me. Within a year, for budgetary reasons, the GM and I were handling all four responsibilities. A year after that, he retired and I became acting GM, all four jobs landing on my desk (though the licensee loaned me someone from their staff part time to help with the office stuff). This meant making programming decisions, writing and composing the monthly program magazine, being on the road seeking corporate support, and interviewing prospects to replace me as Program Director. This was far harder than it had been to produce a television show without help.

One day, when the deadline for getting the program guide to the printer was looming, I was sitting at the word processor, smacking out a heartfelt bit of prose, when one of the announcers appeared in my doorway and asked how the search for a new PD was going. Without turning around, I said we were narrowing it down. There was a brief silence and then he said something that brought me up short. "Well, it'll sure be good to get some leadership around here again." I stopped what I was doing and turned around and looked at the empty doorway and laughed. He was right. In my effort to do everything else right, I was failing at the most important part of the job. I hadn't just ignored my responsibility to lead the staff – I'd stopped being a part of the team.

That's what makes the difference between a station where some people with good voices play music and deliver information, and a broadcasting station in which everybody feels the same rhythm, where the personalities on the air know the people they're working for care about them and back them up. Too many businesses are run by people who fail to remember that the reputation and the survival of the entire corporation rests on the well-being of the guy on the line.

This story ends well. One bright, sunny day, I came back from lunch to find a guy standing in the hallway looking at our teletype machines (thankfully a thing of the past). He was the manager of a local commercial station but, he told me, the first button on his car radio was set to Blue Lake Public Radio. When he learned I was looking for a Program Director, he said he'd like to apply for the job. I was floored. He knew classical music, understood the needs of on-air staff because he'd done that early in his career, had long years of management experience, was familiar with the technical side of broadcasting, and was willing to take a pay cut to work for a station that shared his values. Don't try to convince me that angels don't exist.

Dave Myers and I were both Air Force veterans, had come up the long way in broadcasting, and had the same philosophy about what makes a good station work. In my mind, even though we held different titles, we were co-managers of Blue Lake Public Radio, and some pretty good things took place while we were working together. I managed the budget and took the heat from the licensee and Dave was the idea man. We had a standing joke that every time he stuck his head in my office door, it was going to cost us money. The fact is that when it did, it was always worth it.

Perhaps our most significant achievement during that period was solving the problem of poor reception in parts of Grand Rapids, where many of our member/listeners were. We'd tried a number of fixes and tweaks, all of them useless, even raising the height of our microwave tower that sent the station signal to our Oceana County transmitter. Dave and I valiantly dug the 80-foot trench for the transmission line ourselves on the hottest day of the century. Then one day he appeared with a really expensive idea – and a really good one. He'd discovered that a station in Grand Rapids, owned by Moody Bible Institute of Chicago, might be faltering. With high hopes and our boss's blessing (and a cap on what we could spend), we drove to Chicago. We both remember a cordial meeting, sincere interest on their part in having Blue Lake succeed them as owners of the station, and their agreeing to sell it to us for exactly what we'd determined we could afford. That station became WBLU, sister station to Blue Lake's flagship station, WBLV.

When I retired, Dave took over the corner office, guiding the station to further growth and success, including fulfilling our dream of doubling the size of the building and adding a studio large enough to accommodate a full orchestra. Now he's been succeeded by our mutual friend, Paul Boscarino, another veteran broadcaster, who knows that while very important stuff gets done in the GM's office, the most important part of the operation is what goes on in that other corner of the building, the on-air studio.

At this writing, it's been 32 years since I left television and more than 20 since I retired from Blue Lake Public Radio. It gratifies me that there are still some people who remember my television days. It pleases me even more to encounter so many people who are loyal listeners to Blue Lake Fine Arts Camp's two Public Radio stations, WBLV and WBLU, where the rhythm is as strong in the building as it is on the air.

More Vox Populi...

"Today is Ground Hog Day. As for me, I hope the sleepy little animal prophet does not see his shadow. Who are we to believe, him or Buck Matthews?"

"Winter is gone, Spring is sprung, If Buck Matthews, has anything to do with the weather, He ought to be hung!"

"Old weathermen never die –
They just cloud up and move out to sea."
                    Dar Hollinrake

Llanfairpwllgwyngyllgogerychwyrn-drobwllllantysiliogogoch

A History Lesson for Today

I would very much appreciate a sincere effort to stifle your laughter at the mention of one of the most historic and significant towns in Wales, the musical country that is one of the lands of my origin. (The other two are England and Germany, but neither of them has a town whose name contains 58 letters.) My Gaelic is wanting now for lack of practice, but not so many years ago I could actually pronounce the name, albeit without the Walish accent.

This place is not your average Keokuk or Hamtramk, either. Located on the island of Anglesey, it's been there since 4,000 BC (that's the Neolithic Era, baby) and 3,000 people still live there. They didn't call it **Llanfairpwllgwyngyllgogerychwyrndrobwllllantysiliogogoch** at first. The modest, conservative Walers originally named it **Llanfair Pwllgwyngyll** and it stayed that way for the first 5,860 years. Then some local merchant hit on the idea that it would be good for tourism to have their railroad station bear the longest name in Great Britain. The minutes of the town council meeting in which this brilliant idea was proposed and passed have long since disappeared but it must have been a jolly evening. I suspect a good deal of singing was involved.

And don't think the name has no meaning. It translates to "St. Mary's Church in the hollow of the white hazel near the rapid whirlpool and the Tysilio Parish with a red cave."

When it comes to long, unpronounceable names, the United States has a dog in the fight, too. Thanks to the Nipmuc branch of the Algonquins, there's a lake in Massachusetts the original name of which is **Chargoggagoggmanchauggagoggchaubunagungamaugg** - although the pansies who live around there now call it Webster Lake. The name has been loosely translated to "Fishing place at the boundaries – Neutral fishing grounds." Some of the locals like to say it really means "You fish on your side, I'll fish on my side, and nobody fish in the middle." 45 letters hardly holds its head up in the company of **Llanfairpwll**….. well, you know, that other place – but the Nipmucs did have a couple of things going for them the Welsh couldn't match. In 1954, Decca produced a record of Ethel Merman and Ray Bolger singing a song about the lake – and the Gs in the name outnumber the Welsh 15 to 9.

Tomorrow we'll consider another mighty municipal name, one that makes my Welsh ancestors and the Nipmucs both look absolutely unimaginative. The original name of Bangkok contains *163 letters.*

Waiting

It's normal to think of waiting as a form of inactivity. Sitting, standing, idling – it's a time pf pause between things that happen. For me, waiting is often time spent doing something I might not have time to do otherwise. Reading, usually. This – writing – sometimes. But always wanting the time spent to be time spent usefully. If nothing else avails, I study people or consider how things work or try to discover something new in familiar surroundings.

I've waited a lot – most often in the same circumstances as everyone else - for departure, for the line to move or the light to change. Anticipation can make waiting interesting or frightening or surprising, depending on where and why you're waiting.

Recently, while waiting for my name to be called at the Veterans Administration Clinic, surrounded by my peers, I remembered the painful anticipation of mail call when I was in the Air Force in Korea. Victim of a last name that begins in the middle of the alphabet, I had to endure the 12 letters preceding M before learning, too often, that the waiting was in vain.

Sitting there, watching the old troops passing by brought on many thoughts of the cruelty of time. Once creased and cadenced and waiting for the call, we had all experienced the military's infamous policy of "Hurry up and wait." Now we were reduced to a medley of malfunctions of body, mind, and spirit. Heroes some, reduced to helplessness. Guys who had run toward the action, now limping toward the grave. We are all so different now. A few still lucky to be agile and aware, some wearing their personalities in their cowboy hats and beards, some with fear in their eyes – a new enemy waiting ahead.

And, saddest of all, an occasional young one, damaged beyond repair by the adventure in the Middle East. These, more victim than the rest of us. We went because we believed our going had purpose, something to be gained, even in so great a mystery as war. But these poor kids, waiting with the rest of us, went to fight for a cause that wasn't a cause, for a people who waited for them to leave so the tribal mischief could resume.

I wonder what these young vets must think when they realize that the hell of war has just begun.

Grateful Nation

If you're looking for a slam against the government of the United States, look elsewhere. I am, of course, in agreement with anybody who believes there's much about it that isn't working right, especially the double-partisan Congress. I also believe some of its agencies are failing us in profound and harmful ways. But I refuse to stand with those who think a different system would serve us better, or who think the President isn't doing as well as anyone could, given the opposite party's commitment to blocking anything he attempts to do. Read this as meaning any President, either opposition party.

However, I write this on behalf of the one Federal agency that I deal with frequently, the Department of Veterans Affairs – the VA. Full disclosure: My mother worked for the VA in Washington for more than 25 years. But that was more than 50 years ago, and it's a vastly different agency now. In her day, the VA's caseload hadn't increased substantially since the end of WW1. Today, more than 6,500,000 men and women are active patients.

The deception committed by some VA clinics in covering up life-threatening delays in seeing patients, and the failure of the agency to quickly process applications for care by veterans of the Middle East debacle was immeasurably wrong. But let's don't forget why those things happened. It's pretty hard to operate efficiently when your caseload increases 78% in 14 years and Congress cuts your funding by $1,500,000,000. The people who continue to do the best they can under those circumstances deserve a little understanding.

From a personal standpoint, I can say that the Veterans Administration is a Godsend. I'd been a veteran of military service for more than 40 years before I got around to signing up. I was reluctant to do so because my experience in uniform in no way equated to what these poor kids coming back from Iraq and Afghanistan have been through. I wasn't wounded and I suffered no lasting effects from being in the Korean combat zone. But I was eligible and the cost of my prescription drugs was getting out of hand, so I decided to exercise my benefits.

The care I've received from the VA has been exceptional. My prescription medications are mailed to me at a considerable discount (and a reasonable co-pay), and I'm provided with hearing aids and glasses at no cost. Just as important, the doctors and nurses and specialists are unfailingly polite and respectful and never condescending. And they now have the advantage of providing their services in a new, uncrowded facility in southwest Grand Rapids.

My family has another connection to the VA that precedes my mother's employment there. When the gasses of WW1 finally caught up with him in 1944, my father lived out his last few weeks at the Mt. Alto Veterans Administration Hospital in Washington. At that time, the means for treating a condition like his were rudimentary at best. But he was cared for, as I am today.

They say that veterans' benefits are a grateful nation's debt to those who've served it. All of the veterans I know are grateful to the nation we served for caring about us.

Duty

As one of the lucky ones who emerged from military service intact and functional and privileged to live a full and meaningful life, I'm never unaware of how lucky I've been. Although that experience ended more than sixty years ago, and occupied less than five percent of my life, it's surprising how large it still looms in memory. Many former servicemen and women try hard to forget that period in their lives and with good reason. I want never to forget.

Like my father, who served as a medical corpsman with the storied Rainbow Division in World War I, I was a non-combatant in a combat zone. Unlike him, whose field hospital unit was often under fire while providing first response medical care to soldiers on the line in Europe, I endured no privations other than uncomfortable accommodations and unimaginative food while serving in Korea. I went to work every morning at the communications center, did my six-hour shift in the radio shack, and went "home" to my tent at the end of the day. It wasn't Pleasant Valley – but nobody was shooting at me.

They *were* shooting at the guys we were there to support. The real work force of the Air Force, they were the pilots of the American and South African squadrons attached to the 18th Fighter–Bomber Wing. Their enor-

Charles O. Matthews, Sr.

Charles O. Matthews, Jr.

mous responsibility and the risks they took in fulfilling it humbled those of us who stayed behind on the ground. Day and night, in their nearly obsolete, poorly-armored little Mustangs – hardly bigger than automobiles, they flew continuous interdiction strikes against the North Korean and Chinese supply lines and transport routes. Out they'd go and back – some of them – would come, take on gas and ammunition, and out they'd go again. Such bravery was hard to comprehend.

Yet, they were very much like the rest of us – young, loving life, doing what they'd signed up to do, trying to be good enough to survive it, looking forward to going home. Their ticket home was a hundred missions out and back. Some of them wanted to stay and keep flying, but even they knew the odds were against them.

Too many of them didn't make the Century Club, going down over the target or dying in their chutes from enemy fire. It was a sad sight to watch a ground crew waiting on the flight line beyond the reasonable time to expect their bird to return, knowing that the captain of their team was gone. Ordinary men doing extraordinary things – guys who in better times would have, like me, grown old watching the world turn.

Although I know there are legitimate conscientious reasons for objecting to war, I've always believed that military service is an experience that all young men should have, whether in peacetime or when the country is at war. I think patriotism requires more than just standing when the flag goes by. That kind of duty is both ennobling and enriching because it requires you to think and work collectively for a common cause. And it often places you in the company of people who, like the Mustang drivers of the 18th Fighter-Bomber Wing, rise above their own expectations and become heroes.

The Colors

Anyone who's ever worn the uniform of the United States knows that the proper name for the flag of our country is, "The Colors." We honor the fabric, we fight for The Colors. It's always bothered me that you have to be a member of the armed services to learn that respect for the flag is as important as paying your taxes and obeying the law.

Who doesn't get mad at how we do things in this country from time to time? For all the good we've done in the world, we've also managed to embarrass ourselves in grand style now and then. There are lots of ways to express outrage at the dumb stuff done by Congress or the President or the major parties, or on any of the thorny issues that have us bristling from time to time. It's our right as citizens of a free land. But there's no justification for abusing The Colors. To do so – by burning them, or walking on them, or ripping them up, or spitting on them, or any of the several criminally insensitive ways the whiners think of to publicly suck their thumbs – is just clear evidence of an arrogant lack of gratitude for the privilege of living in a country that doesn't shoot you for being a dissident – or for just being a hypocritical ass, for that matter.

There's a lesson to be learned about the importance of respect for The Colors from an event, chronicled by the poet John Greenleaf Whittier, that took place in 1864 in the little farm community of Frederick, Maryland, during the War Between the States. Time was when every grade school kid in the country had to recite it, but there may not be any teachers left who've even heard of it.

Whittier's poem, *The Ballad of Barbara Frietchie*, paints a picture of Stonewall Jackson's Rebel troops marching through town, spotting a Union flag flying from the attic window of the 30-year-old seamstress. According to Whittier, the troops fired on the flag, which brought Barbara to the window with the challenge to shoot her – "but spare your country's flag!"

Righteous, weary, and angry though they were, fighting at the time under another flag, the Confederates were also honorable men. Led most likely by General A. P. Hill, they saluted her – and The Colors – and marched on, most of them to die the following day at Antietam.

Woodrow Wilson said of our flag, "It is the emblem of our unity, our power, our thoughts and purpose as a nation." So, let's cut the crap about desecrating the flag being a legitimate expression of free speech. Too many good men and women have died to keep it flying. They respected it and so should the rest of us.

Flower Girl
A Story of War

She was, as is often the case with the nouveau riche, overdressed. The woolen jumper and rubber shoes were just too much for August. The outfit, in those surroundings, was comical – but in that punishing afternoon heat and suspended dust, her smile and the peach-colored plastic rose pinned to her breast almost redeemed an otherwise colorless world.

The wide intersection of the two gravel roads was the center point of a town that might once have been serene and beautiful. Through the dusty trees, one could see the distant granite heights, from which the watered terraces descended into the verdant valley. Here, by the shallow river, the world had come to find Chinhae. The ancient footpaths which crossed here had widened to become two highways, one of which ran straight north, into the war. The traffic, too, had changed into an odd mix of oxcarts and weapons carriers and women with babies on their backs and six-bys loaded with green troops.

I backed the big, open staff car into the retreating shade of an enormous oriental pine. It had, I was sure, seen such comings and goings for a hundred years. I rested my chin on my hands, still atop the wheel, and watched the poor little rich girl move about the crowded square – pausing here to speak with an old papa-san squatting on his rice mat, waving away the flies – and again to accept a gift of candy from a soldier loafing by the village shrine.

She moved toward me slowly, my curiosity rising as her image came more clearly into focus through the dirty windshield. I lowered the glass to the hood to get a better view and take her picture. Attracted by the motion, she saw me with the camera and struck a pose, waiting for me to wind and shoot again. She tossed a

Korea 1952

little wave and darted out of sight behind the tree. I wondered how one so young could look so old.

The other children in the square, beggars and pimps and hustlers, were upon me then, little wolves in a noisy, nasty pack.

"Hey, GI, you richsumbitch, got big car, you General, right? Hey, you got plenty money! Hey, we steal car, go ride, okay?" The din was awful and so was their need. I waved them off with mock threats and they moved away.

All but one. He'd bumped into the running board of the big open vehicle as the others jangoed off. He stood there, confused, almost naked, leaning on a withered leg, cheeks streaked beneath his sightless eyes. It was too much. I pulled a food bar from my ration pack and pressed it into his pleading hand. "Here, pal. Eat this quick before the other animals spot it."

His aim was remarkably good for a blind cripple. The ration hit me just above the left eye, leaving a small scratch I would feel for two days. The withered leg and the blind eyes healed miraculously as he bounded away down the road to catch up with his companions. "Run, you little shit!"

Then, she was in front of me, her little hand extended, holding the rejected gift out to me. She looked younger than she was, I thought. Seven, maybe. Eight at the outside. She looked as wise as the old man dozing on his mat. *They've all seen too much. What the hell is this all about?* The universal question of the enlisted man. *What does any of this do for these people?* Nobody wants us here but us. Fulfill the mission, kick a little ass, and send another truckload to the front.

"Here, GI. Boy-san throw this." The voice was thin and tired. I pushed the ration back to her.

"No, honey. You keep it. If you're not hungry, save it for later. Good stuff." I rubbed my stomach for emphasis.

The bar disappeared inside the hand-me-down jumper. *Wouldn't the Park Avenue broad who pitched that outfit choke if she could see it now?* I wondered if she'd have understood the irony, the connecting joy her casual altruism had brought to her privileged daughter and to this pitiful child of war. The little face smiled up at me. Just that. No hustle. Just casing me, assessing the possibilities.

"What's your name, jo-san?"

"Betty Lou, GI." The name came with the clothes. Some wise ass Red Cross khaki boy must have tagged her with that one because he was too lazy to attempt her Korean name.

"No, jo-san. Your Korean name."

Very clearly and distinctly, she pronounced her name for me. "Nanjiku, GI."

I looked at her carefully and worked it over in my mind. When I attempted to repeat her name, it came out more like "Nancy Girl." I said it again the same way, more convinced that we might settle for that. "Nancy Girl. How's that?"

She looked at me with those round brown eyes and granted me no such permission. "Nanjiku, GI. Say Nahn – Jee – Koo."

"Okay, Teach. Nahn – jee – koo. No Nancy Girl. No Betty Lou, either."

"Okay, no Betty Lou."

"You all alone, Nanjiku?" She was puzzled by that. "Alone? You know, you have no family?"

"No family. Why you ask that? You want mama-san? No mama-san, GI." She looked hurt. She'd also spent too much time around the little pimps who hustled for their destitute, desperate mothers.

"No, no, Nanjiku." I cared that she not think of me as just another carpet-bagger, fornicating my way through the Land of the Morning Calm.

"Mama-san dead, GI." The smile faded slightly. She looked down. More softly, she said, "Papa-san dead, too. All dead."

The word came without passion or grief, as if she was just telling me their ages. No tears – had she ever cried? How did she react when the napalm or the shell or the crossfire had left the pieces of her family quivering in the dust? Had she, like others I'd seen, just looked up steadily at whoever was responsible and left a mark a lifetime of regret would not erase?

My attention was distracted briefly by a commotion near the gate of the house where the CO was conducting his afternoon "inspection." Two MPs had collared an AWOL and were reorganizing his shape so it would fold into the back seat of a Jeep. When I looked again, she wasn't there.

"Hey, GI," the little voice said from behind me. "Let's go!" She was in the shotgun seat, hands folded in her lap, her little legs straight out in front of her. "Come on, GI. Take Nanjiku for ride!"

The relief I felt surprised me. *This kid is five minutes into my life and I'm glad she's there?*

"Hey, I thought you ran off. I can't take you for ride, Nanjiku. Not my car."

She cocked her head at that. "You steal, GI?"

"No," I laughed. "I no steal. This is honcho's car."

"Why you drive honcho car? Where honcho?" she asked.

Her gaze moved past me and refocused on the whorehouse gate. She smiled again. "Ah, so! Honcho go see Geisha!" I was grateful that she seemed unaware of what really went on behind that gate. She looked at me steadily and asked, "What you name, GI?"

The change in topic was welcome. "My name James, Nanjiku."

"Ah, Jems. Okay. How you do, Jems?" She offered her hand and I shook it, not bothering to correct her pronunciation.

"No ride, Jems? Poor Nanjiku. No ride." Enough like the other little bandits to play the sympathy game. *They're all graduate psychologists, these kids. No wonder they don't starve.*

"Yes, poor Nanjiku. War is hell, right?" *Jesus, what am I saying?* "Okay, kiddo. You got it. Hang on." I turned the big engine over and pulled out into traffic. I swung wide to get around an oxcart plodding into the square from the bridge road and left a roostertail of dust as we rolled south along the Main Supply Route. Nanjiku screamed, experiencing for the first time the intoxicating joy of harmless fear. I glanced at her and saw a child on a roller coaster, tiny hands gripping the sides of the seat, black hair whipping about her face, eyes wide with the wonder of it all – and it struck me that this just might be the only time in her life she's been happy.

About a mile south of the village, I took a wide U turn and headed back into town. The whole trip took less than three minutes but it must have seemed like a trip around the world to the orphan girl. She threw her arms around my neck and squeezed with surprising strength as I again backed into the spot beneath the ancient evergreen.

"Oh, Jems! You Number One!"

"More like number nine if the Old Man had seen that!" I picked up the camera again and turned to catch her laughing.

She reached for the camera. "Nanjiku take picture Jems, okay?"

"Sure, kid. Look through little window. When you see me, push here, easy."

Camera to her eye, mouth screwed into a little half chew, she sighted and fired. "Jems pretty!"

I wheeled at the sound of a shout from the direction of the whorehouse. Straightening his gig line as he stepped over the ditch, the CO yelled, "Get that goddammed gook out of the car!"

"Yessir," I muttered and turned back to the child. She was gone – and so was my camera.

I jumped onto the hood and looked in all directions but she was not to be seen. I dropped to the ground and ran around the big tree – but she wasn't hiding back there, either. She'd disappeared – for good, I thought.

"Why'd you have to yell like that, Colonel? She ran off with my camera."

He grimaced as he dropped into the seat where the child had been sitting. "Well, you can't trust these little bastards. And watch your mouth, Sergeant! I still have your papers to sign. You don't want me to suddenly declare you essential, do you?"

"Sorry, Colonel. I don't think she meant to steal it, sir. Just got scared and took off when you hollered, that's all."

"If you were dumb enough to let her get her hands on it, don't bitch to me." I wondered if he'd remember this later when he came down with some uniquely Oriental disease, obtained from someone he'd trusted during his "inspection."

The ride back to base was pretty quiet. Apparently, the CO had "inspected" the whorehouse thoroughly because he kept falling asleep. Every once in awhile, he'd straighten up and give me a glassy look, then crap out again. I almost lost him on a curve and had to grab a fist full of gabardine, after which he spent a little more time than seemed necessary smoothing out the wrinkles in his sleeve.

When we cleared the gate, I made a coughing noise to get his attention. "Sir, do you mind if I take the car back to town to look for my camera?" He threw his head back far enough to allow him to see me from under the visor of his garrison cap. He squinted at me and grinned. "Okay, son. Take off – but be back here first thing in the morning. I don't want to have to send a search party out to look for your remains. I don't think your family would like you coming home in a rubber sack." He swung out of the vehicle as I braked in front of his quarters, then turned to face me again. "And if you decide to look for your camera at the Palace of Great Delights, ask for the one they call 'Alice.' She's not shopworn yet. And good luck, Sarge."

I had second thoughts about having to worry about the security of the old man's staff car while I played detective in the village, so I dropped it off at the Battalion motor pool and hitched a ride into town on the trash detail truck. I went to the spot where she first appeared and leaned for a time against the gnarled tree trunk, looking for signs of her.

She wasn't in sight and nobody I asked could remember seeing her. Natives circling the wagons. The Koreans were polite and forgiving about our trampling their country, but they were rightly wary of our motives as individuals. Too many of them had been cheated and abused by the screwballs among us. It was almost as if I had imagined her. Only the old papa-san, still sitting cross-legged on his rice-straw mat, smoking his long, thin bamboo pipe, gave me reason to hope.

"Papa-san. You see jo-san? This big," – I held my right hand, palm down, about three feet from the ground – "name Nanjiku?"

He nodded his head in complete agreement with anything I said to him. *Deaf. What else?* But I remembered that he and the child had conversed earlier and there appeared no sign of hearing difficulty, even with the traffic nearby. I pushed. "Papa-san! Where Nanjiku go?" His expression altered only slightly, the cracked and yellow teeth approximating a smile his eyes did not share.

"No see jo-san, GI." His eyes clouded as he looked away. I followed his gaze, across the road to the stalls of the market place and thought I saw her watching us. But the child standing there was wearing native clothing, not the discarded Stateside outfit I'd seen on Nanjiku. The old man did not look at me again, but I sensed he knew something and there was no way I would get it out of him. And I wasn't down to kicking old men around yet.

The heat in the market place was worse than in the open street, intensified by the lack of air circulation and the body heat of the undulating mob of people shopping for the necessities of life. In place of the dust, there hung over the area the oppressive stench of fish and octopus drying in the dying sunlight and the waste of pigs and puppies, both Korean delicacies, churned into a sort of slippery paste underfoot. A hundred tiny stalls, depending on each other for support, displayed a variety of contraband, like a garage sale in a supply depot. Moving through the narrow aisles, I brushed away the eager hands pressing bargains upon me. Not only was it illegal to sell such items but equally so to purchase them The occasional MP raid was thwarted by the mysterious market telegraph, which spread the warning well ahead of the white helmets. All they ever saw was produce, fish , and handcrafted items where minutes before had been displayed ammo cases, gun belts, canteens, GI field jackets, combat boots, and cameras.

I nearly forgot my mission, so caught up was I in the almost surreal atmosphere of the market. I raised my eyes to look along the double row of stalls and take in the oppressive beauty of it all. Except for the circumstance of war, here was the essence of the Orient. Life going on, no matter what. I thought of Faulkner's observation that man will not merely survive – he will prevail – and knew that no matter how much we toyed with the history of this place, a thousand years beyond our lives, these people would still be swaying with the winds of time.

Then I was certain she was there, near the last stall on the right. I couldn't see her face or form but the peach color of the plastic rose burned through the shadowing canvas world like a roman candle. I broke into a sort of running walk, the best I could manage in competition with the sauntering service men and chattering natives, toward the place where I thought I saw her.

The closer I got, the more I doubted myself and the faster I tried to move. Nearly there, I dodged a woman carrying a nursing baby and slipped in the dung underfoot. I started to go down but my fall was broken by hands that caught me under the arms from behind.

"What's the hurry, Sarge? You're gonna mess up your class A's if you ain't careful." Two military cops patrolling the market.

Ignoring them for the moment, I turned quickly to where Nanjiku's flower had been and saw, instead, a tin pan filled with freshly harvested fish roe. Even this close, the colors were the same. In frustration, I wheeled back to the MPs and exclaimed, "Goddammit, she was there, I know she was!"

The two men exchanged smiles. "Right, Sarge. No doubt about it. What's the problem, lose your girlfriend?" They thought I was drunk.

"Oh, hell, I'm just looking for a kid who lifted my camera this afternoon. I thought I saw her in here."

The lower rank of the two moved closer, as if to check my breath. "Okay, you want some help sweepin' the place? What's she look like? As if that would help. They all look alike."

"Not this one – and, yeah, that would be great. She's maybe seven or eight, wearing a dark blue stateside dress with a plastic flower on the front. She might be carrying a C3, but she may already have hocked it."

"You're chasin' a kid because she took off with an Argus C3? Why bother? You can buy one of those pieces of shit at half a dozen stalls right in here for about fifteen bucks."

"Well, I want mine back because it's still got a roll of film in it I don't wanta lose. I'm rotating in a couple of weeks."

"You really want something to remind you of this hell-hole? Man, I'd let it go."

Nevertheless, the two MPs did help me look for the kid in the market, each of us taking an aisle and moving through deliberately, checking under the tables and stands as we went. The merchants observed me carefully. They knew I wasn't shopping and made no move to sell me any of their wares. Neither did they offer any knowledge of the child.

We emerged at about the same time, empty-handed. I thanked the two GI cops, who volunteered to contact me at the outfit if they spotted the child. I stood and watched them get into their Jeep and drive away slowly toward the south, wishing I had the authority to commandeer them to continue the search. I turned and walked past the whorehouse gate toward the intersection. I was sweating from the awful heat and the anxiety of the whole event. I felt suddenly weak and tired and sorry I hadn't brought the staff car into the village so I could just get the hell out of there. Screw the camera. Like the MP said, I could get a knock-off in the market for fifteen or twenty bucks or I could get the genuine article for sixty-eight dollars at the PX in Tokyo when I cleared through. I checked the traffic for a ride back to Battalion.

My resolve returned instantly, for there she was in the middle of the road, in the company of the old papa-san, the two of them weaving their way in my direction, running as fast as her short legs and his bony old frame would allow. He had his mat rolled up beneath one arm and in his other hand was my camera. The old son-of-a-gun, I thought. He's found her and is bringing my camera back to me. I knew he wasn't as dumb as he pretended.

In my delight, I yelled to her. "Nanjiku!" They both looked up, surprised. Nanjiku smiled broadly but the old man grimly yanked her hand and turned away from me, toward the bridge road westward. I yelled again just before they made it to the corner building and out of sight. "NAN-JIKU, WAIT!"

I ran to the corner and turned to see them cresting the bridge, headed for the vast, squalid cluster of makeshift shanties where most of the displaced natives lived. I heard her little voice raised in protest, though not in fear, and the one word spoken in English – "Jems!" A few steps more and they were gone.

It was almost life-threatening to run in that heat but I had no choice. Once inside that shacktown, they could vanish unless I get there while the track was warm. I made it to the center of the bridge and had to stop for breath. The hopelessness of it all overtook me there and I slumped against the concrete rail, scanning the native quarter in hopes that they might return. Nothing.

In the riverbed below, I could hear the gossip of the old women, busy doing laundry in the only source of drinking water they had. I watched the yellow water curl from rock to pool through miniature canyons, conveying little ships of battle trash, survivors of the long trip south. At one point, the water shallowed through the broken carcass of a camera, it's shattered lens staring blindly at the sun.

Well, that takes care of that. The old bastard deep-sixed the evidence on the run. I wondered what it would feel like if I caught the son-of-a-bitch and dropped his skinny ass off that bridge. I regretted the thought immediately. I had to admire the old man for protecting the child. My mood had been anything but benevolent when I questioned him – and Americans were not known for their kindness in the country. For all he knew, Nanjiku was in danger. At least, we had that in common.

The longer I stood there, the more futile the whole thing seemed. I had come to retrieve my camera and it was now junk in the riverbed. What would be the point of my going into the shanties in search of the child? *Maybe, Jems, it wasn't the camera you were after. Admit it. It was the kid, wasn't it?* I was suddenly aware that I wanted to see that little girl again – but for what? What could I do with her if I found her? I couldn't adopt her – I was heading home in two weeks. I couldn't take her on base with me. The irony stirred my stomach. If she was ten years older and looking at me through a gunsight, I could have killed her. But she was a little girl, looking at me through those pleading eyes and I couldn't save her.

So long, kid. I pushed away from the bridge rail and turned toward the intersection, moving resolutely away from the frustration I felt, more sure with every step that the child was best forgotten. I crossed the road and waited to hitch a ride back to Battalion. Watching the northbound traffic, I saw the MP Jeep slowly turn the corner westward, heading toward the bridge.

I hesitated only a moment, then ran into the road and flagged them down. "Hey, Sarge, did you find your little thief?"

"Not yet, but I saw her go into the shantytown a little while ago. You have time to give me some more help?"

"Oh, hell yeah. Nothin' else is goin' on and nobody's drunk enough to haul in. Let's do it."

We poked our heads into every little shack in the area, getting more tired with every step. I felt guilty for intruding even momentarily on the privacy of the little family groups gathered inside them, imagining how they must feel to know that not even there could they escape the monumental presence of American soldiers.

"Enough of this, you guys. Let's give it up. Can you give me a lift back to base?"

We were almost back to the Jeep when one of the MPs said, "I'll be damned. Sarge, you ain't gonna believe this!" I looked over his shoulder and saw what surprised him. There, sitting in the back seat of the military police vehicle was Nanjiku, smiling broadly, and holding my camera in her little hand. "Jems! Smile!"

Oh, I did. And so did the MPs. They reacted as if they'd just solved a case, high-fiving each other and slapping me on the back. One of them had a passable knowledge of street Korean and interpreted for me as I tried to learn as much as possible about the little girl. It turned out the old papa-san, who'd known her family, was doing his best to protect her, providing a place for her to eat and sleep.

She guided us to his shanty, where I did my best to persuade him to let her go into one of the orphan schools being run by volunteers in Chinhae. I could hardly blame him for being suspicious of a stranger who might not have her best interests at heart. He did agree to meet with a civilian representative, who would be able, I hoped, to convince him of the advantages she'd have in their care.

I discovered, however, that the orphanages were already overflowing, with hardly enough resources to feed and clothe the kids they had. But I was able to get a Korean teacher, who spoke better English than I did, to come with me and talk with Ninjiku and her protector. In the end, they worked it out and a few days before I shipped out, I visited her at the school and told her that I would never forget her and we would always be friends.

"Oh, Jems – you be my papa-san? Why you go away?"

I asked the teacher to tell her for me that she could think of me as her uncle and that I would stay in touch. I would always want to know how she was doing. I hoped she'd learn to write and send me letters and pictures. I gave the teacher my camera and asked that she give it to Ninjiku when she thought it would be safe for her to have it. I also promised that I would do my best to provide the money for her education as time went along.

Leaving Korea was harder than leaving home to go there had been. The little girl with the plastic flower on her dress had won my heart and I cried unashamedly as the plane lifted off the runway, headed for Japan and the ship that would take me back to the States.

That was sixty years ago. Nanjiku survived the war and went on to have a good life, marrying and raising a daughter of her own. We did stay in touch and I have many photos she took with my old Argus C3. Now an educated woman with a career in social work, she still calls me "Jems."

She named her daughter "Nancy."

Garden of Stone

Hallowed Ground

Among the nation's most revered places is Arlington National Cemetery, across the Potomac River from Washington, DC. It is the resting place of some 400,000 military dead, from all wars and all branches of service. If it's true that home is wherever your parents are, then in a poetic sense, Arlington is my home because two of those graves, located near the Confederate Memorial on Jackson Circle in Section 16, are occupied by my mother and father.

There is something about our National Cemeteries, wherever they are, that is so serene, so dignified, so respectful of the men and women memorialized there that it's impossible not to feel their presence. In those sacred places, it is the very uniformity and order that contributes to their serenity. The ranks and files of identical stones speak of the tradition and discipline of military service. It's what they knew when they were alive. It reflects the brotherhood of the uniform.

All of this is in place tenfold at our most honored National Cemetery in Arlington, Virginia. Before it became my father's resting place, I had been there several times for Easter sunrise services and other events in the amphitheater. It was meaningful to me even then because I knew the time would come when Pop would be reunited with his Rainbow Division comrades.

Arlington National Cementary

I wish every American could spend some time there and feel the power and hear the message in those 400,000 white marble headstones in perfect rows across the rolling, tree-lined hills. To watch the lone sentry pacing the terrace before the Grave of the Unknown Soldier – night and day, in any weather; to hear the cadenced footsteps of the Honor Guards; to see the six-horse teams pulling the caissons and their flag-draped caskets; to watch the lone horse with boots reversed in the stirrups following the procession; to hear the rifle volleys and the heartbreaking sound of "Taps" over the graves; to observe the incredible respect with which the uniformed pall bearers fold the flags in perfect triangles and present them to the next of kin – to see all that and not be moved is simply not possible.

My father went to rest there in 1944, just when American troops were once again storming ashore to save France. Fifty-two years later, my mother joined him, their adjacent graves now shaded by an old-growth flowering bush. Across the access road, in the circle that contains the graves of Confederate soldiers, the old monument bears these words, written by a Confederate officer who became an Episcopal priest in Washington following the Civil War:

"Not for fame or reward, not for place or for rank,
Not lured by ambition or goaded by necessity,
But in simple obedience to duty as they understood it,
These men suffered all, sacrificed all, dared all – and died."

The Haunted Month

The seasons of the year march past me in their coats of many colors,
    paced by sounds and rhythms unique to each,
        trailing aromatic signatures as identifiable as fingerprints.

They impress and amuse me in their individual ways -
    and, just as I would show respect for the flags of other nations,
        I acknowledge their leafy pennants snapping in the breeze.

The clink and rattle of late winter ice in tree and bush,
    the hoof beat cadence of spring rainstorms passing by,
        the polished brass of summer sunshine in my eye,
            the painted glory of autumnal color guards
                all inspire dreams of my own season not yet in view.

I watch impatiently the oncoming parade of seasons and events.
    Here's my birthday,
        there is Easter,
            here comes Independence Day.

All familiar and alluring,
    but far removed from those late yearly changes in the sky,
        new flavors in the air,
            and stray feathers from no bird I ever knew.

But it's coming, I can tell.
    Halloween drifts by,
        here comes Thanksgiving Day.
            Then, just as the pace quickens,
                time slows and November's last six days
                    cling to each other like people on a sinking ship.

Still it comes.
    I can feel the rustle that precedes it.
        My body clock signals the impending solstice. –

Then suddenly there washes over me the wonderful inevitability of it all.
It's here!
    Like a good book too long unopened,
        December has come back to fill my heart with whispers
            from the past.

I've known joy in every season.
    I could write songs about the sweetness in every other month.
        but only in December do the ghosts of childhood Christmases
            return to rattle softly on the shutters of my memories

And, as I was in those long ago days
    when I was sure he was keeping a list,
        I am purified.
        It's December!

There's no reason to forget that for a time when I was young
    our family endured, as did the Cratchits, near privation.
        But not at Christmas.

I didn't know then the yearly miracle my parents wrought
    in giving us the means to celebrate so grandly at the birthday
        of the King.
            Surrounded by a loving family,
                we feasted and laughed and carried on as if tomorrow
                had been cancelled.

December's ghosts remind me, too,
    of keeping that joy alive after my father died.
        We thought we couldn't do it, but we did.

My mother's strength and love and her determination
    to keep her grief from tarnishing those tinseled days –
        and the undeniable presence of my father's spirit in the
        midst of it all –
            made sure the Yuletide would continue to ring.

And even with the passage of time
    and the departure of all those
        with whom I shared those marvelous times,
            those memories come to life again every December
                in a unique and precious way.

Three hundred sixty-four times a year,
 breakfast is for me no more than a mindless obligation.
  But once – one glorious once each December,
   I go to the table with my senses finely tuned,
    ready for a meal that pays homage
     to a higher master than my stomach.

In our house, as in our scattered tribe,
 Christmas breakfast has always been oyster stew,
  a tradition that has never been broken.
   Even when I was in Korea,
    my mother sent me a can of oyster stew
     and a box of oyster crackers.

It tasted nearly as good from my canteen cup as it does
 from Franciscan ware.

So, whatever winter brings,
 my December every year provides me with a stage
  on which my Christmas ghosts
   can play and replay and play yet once again
    those flickering yesterdays on which my tomorrows are built.

After all, December is the beginning of what's to come.

Listening

Through the closed door, I hear the muffled laughter
    Of the television enjoying itself.
Through the open window, I hear the raucous joy
    Of Spring awakening again.
The lipstick and the Lincolns sell themselves,
    The crickets celebrate each other.
The news flashes, a branch crashes,
    And my heart moves closer to the window.

The Christmas Gift

Every Christmas season brings back another memory that warms my heart. The year was 1948 and I was in the first semester of my freshman year at Ohio Wesleyan University. Not yet sure of my direction in life, college, like high school, was a thrill that failed to instill in me sufficient interest in getting an education. I gloried in the extracurricular aspects of campus life but rarely felt at home among the students who'd arrived there with more purpose.

Christmas break came and I needed to go back home to discover why I'd gone in the first place. So, along with a few other students from the Washington area, I boarded the old Trailways bus with more baggage in my heart than in my suitcase. I sat alone, my eyes half-focused on the world beyond the rain-streaked window, wondering if I really wanted to come back to Ohio.

Somewhere along old Route 40, the bang and rattle of the bus began to soften some and I became aware that the road sounds were muffled because the rain had turned to snow flurries, then snow, and then blizzard conditions. Even the sleepiest among us was wide awake then, aware that the driver was having increasing difficulty in seeing the road and, finally, making headway against the winter storm. Finally, he gave up, pulled over onto what he hoped was the shoulder and announced that until conditions improved, he didn't want to risk our lives by continuing. We were stranded and alone atop a mountain pass, the wind-driven snow drifting against the idling bus.

For each of us, homebound for the holidays, there were a few moments of caution and regret, and no shortage of fear that we might not be rescued before the gas ran out and the heaters failed. It grew very quiet again as everyone aboard grappled with his own set of concerns – and then a most remarkable thing happened. Without anyone taking the lead, that we're-all-in-this-together thing took over and we simply began to enjoy the experience. We sang carols, laughed at stuff that wouldn't have been funny anyplace else. We shared in the Christmas cookies and fruitcakes on board, and we marveled at the frightening beauty of the landscape the blizzard was creating.

Sometime around 3 or 4 in the morning, the frivolity calmed and people began to fall asleep or just back into their reveries. Some chatted with the driver while some others listened for but secretly hoped not to hear the sound of plows or wreckers that might have been dispatched to get us to shelter. Eventually, the only sound was the idling engine and the whir of the heater fans.

Then, out of the dark near the rear of the bus, a single, beautiful voice arose – a clear, sweet soprano singing a song I'd never heard before. Gradually, the whole bus came awake and our spirits rose with the sound of that beautiful melody in that strange, shared place. When the song was finished, the silence remained as we all came to understand that we might have just received an unexpected gift. Not long after that, the storm abated, the plows arrived, the road was cleared and we arrived in Washington safely later in the day.

I suspect that each year as Christmas comes, everyone still alive who was on that bus that stormy night is still haunted, as I am, by the memory of the magic moment when Wesleyan freshman Kathleen Perkins calmed the storm with "I Wonder as I Wander," based on an Appalachian folk melody. It is, truly, a gift that keeps on giving.

If I Had My Life to Live Over...

It's pretty amazing how many people reach the end of their lives and look back with something other than contentment with how things turned out. There's a lot of lamenting over missed opportunities, bad choices, wrong turns, mistakes made and regrets about relationships lost. It's true even of people whose lives have been interesting and fruitful, yet who wish they could rewind their lives to some point and have a do-over. Me, too – sort of.

Well, actually, for me it's not so much that I'd like to go back and change anything as it is to wonder where I might be now if certain things had turned out differently.

Take college, for example. Had I stuck it out the first time around and earned a degree in one of my then areas of interest, such as the ministry or audio visual education, would I have become a preacher or an instructor or a producer?

I was proud to serve in the Air Force and I did well as a ground radio operator and, later, as a communications instructor. I was a Staff Sergeant by the end of my hitch and was recommended for Officers Candidate School. A military career had some appeal for me. I'd have seen a good deal of the world, and still been young enough to pursue a civilian career when I retired.

When radio happened to me, I thought it was more excitement than a boy should have. I envisioned a swift upward curve to the big leagues – and, as written in other parts of this book, it seemed as if that would happen. Starting at little one-lung stations in Michigan and New Jersey, I'd landed a high-profile job at one of the country's premier stations. Had I not been fired there, might I have made it to the networks?

Getting into television in a small market, then moving up to a more important market like Grand Rapids was extremely satisfying. By then, though, I'd come to my senses and actually had no ambition to move to the big markets, even though I received an invitation from CBS in New York. I've wondered what that might have been like, and what it could have led to.

Well, there's no need to speculate on how my life would have differed had I stuck it out in college. The twin discoveries of the rocky path to ministry and the plain hard work when you get there were enough to make any calling I thought I had evaporate like steam.

By the time I got back from Korea and had reached the time for a decision about staying in the service, I'd heard the siren song of show business, which appealed to me a great deal more.

A network radio job, exciting and lucrative as that might have been, would also have put me, far too early in my career, in competition with people of such experience and talent that I'd have gotten neck strain from looking over my shoulder.

And even though the offer from CBS came later in my career when I had more confidence in myself and sufficient experience to know what I was doing, I also knew I was a Midwest sort of guy. Sure, maybe like Phil Donahue, I'd have married a movie star (wink, wink) but I already knew how unpleasant New York City was, and how cut throat the business could be. I'd be moving from a community where I was well-known and accepted, to a place where I'd be a complete unknown. Instead of wondering how exciting the big-time might be, I worried about what would happen if they didn't like me.

So, yeah, maybe life would have been a little different if I'd taken other paths, but I'll never know. What's more important is that, though I certainly could have worked harder at being a better person, I'm happy with the way things turned out and I'm grateful that despite the stupid things I've done, I've managed to make a living and stay out of jail.

You get one shot at life. At least, I hope so. The idea of reincarnation scares the pants off me. What if I came back as a doorknob or a skunk or a robin? Yeah, there's the life – getting your head twisted 50 times a day, having people avoid you all your life, living on worms? I don't think so. Even coming back as myself, facing the same opportunities and choices, doesn't appeal to me at all. I gratefully embrace the philosophy of Been-There-Done-That. Once around is enough for me.

But wait. There is this one other thing. I wouldn't have minded being one of those guys on the History Channel show, *American Pickers*, who've made a career out of crawling around in other people's barns, buying other people's junk.

Nah. Real show business has been way more fun.

Passing Fancy

And now, folks, it's time for the elephant in the room. There are 15 or more words in the English language by which it can be called, but none of them can pave over the fact that we are hurtling toward the end. Try as we may, there's no escaping the fact that life is a borrowed condition and we'll have to give it back. Depending on how we've used it and how it's abused us, some of us might not be all that broken up about trading it in – but that's a topic for someone else's book.

One of the landmarks along the road from youth to, you know, is the fact that, eventually, there are more funerals than weddings to attend. I never liked weddings that much, but I was at least comforted by the *beginnings* implied. And they got pretty entertaining for awhile during the Aquarius phase when the betrothed were creating their own ceremonies. You never knew when they might throw down and boogie their way into the future. But that passed and we got back to tapping our glasses at the reception, and we stopped losing sleep over whether white was the appropriate dress color.

This isn't about the end of life itself but, rather, how it's acknowledged - the rituals we employ to wave goodbye to our loved ones. I once wrote a magazine piece on this subject after returning from a terribly short funeral for an old car friend in Lansing. So short, in fact (parking lot to parking lot in *ten minutes*), I thought it worthy of the Guinness book. The clergyman actually said, between the verses, that there would be no eulogy. Thank you for coming, drive safely.

It's possible, I suppose, that this person, who was a successful, generous businessman, was not so regarded by his survivors. I don't believe that for a minute. To old car cranks like me, he was a saint, because as a sideline, his company made replacement parts for early Chevrolets. He was a very nice guy. But you never know.

The fact is that funerals have changed greatly. Granted, not many are so abbreviated as that one, and I now only attend those for friends and acquaintances about whom there is much to say. But I notice that more and more frequently, the departed are choosing not to be there for the send-off. In fact, there aren't many actual funerals these days. Instead, we have celebrations of life. Nothing wrong with replacing the maudlin organ music with spirited singing, and limiting the time devoted to dreary intonations in favor of laughter – and crying - over the honored one's place in our lives. I just like it better when the person we're cheering on also shows up.

I'm not putting any pressure on my family about this, and I've made it clear that my ghostly form won't be tapping on their window glass at night if my wishes aren't granted. My wife and I have already decided to be cremated and it's entirely up to the family to decide what they do with what's left of me. A mason jar in the strawberry patch, I don't care. But I'd really like to be there for the going away party and have people stop at the box and look down and say things like, "I'm surprised he lasted this long," or "That's a waste of a good suit." A little Dixieland and yodeling would be nice. A band playing "Stars and Stripes Forever," with emphasis on the whump-whumps. A good Methodist lunch. A last ride around the parking lot in an old Chevy.

And, certainly, a recording of my wife and daughter singing the one song I wrote years ago, "I've Had the Best There Is." Because oh, dear friends, I certainly have.

I've always believed that everyone has a song in his heart
just waiting to be written.
This is mine.

Best There Is[*]

The summer is gone with its fields of flowers
And its long, sweet, bright afternoons.
Those warm and enjoyable evening hours
Have all passed a way too soon.

'Tis autumn now, then winter will be upon the land,
But keeping its promise to us once more
Virgin Spring will come again.

The days and the seasons and years have flown
Like the autumn leaves on the breeze,
The people and places and times I've known
Were like ships upon the seas.

And now and then it haunts me, the cycle has an end.
If this is the last time around for me,
What is left for me to spend?

If I had the chance to begin again,
And to change my life in some way,
I would still do the same things I've done so far,
For they've brought me here today.

I'd want the same friends 'round me, the same good family.
How could I improve any part of this?
For I've had the best there is.

And now and then it haunts me, each cycle has an end.
But I wouldn't change any part of this,
For I have the best there is.

*Lyrics written in 1983 for the Japanese folk tune, "Song of the Sea"
Performed often by "Cornsilk" – Thelma and Kim Matthews

Acknowledgements

As people come and go in our lives, they always leave something of themselves with us. This book would never have seen the light of day without the accumulation of what these people contributed to my life. Their encouragement and assistance was the reason I felt brave enough to risk the revelations you've just read. These are some of the special people who helped me get here.

My Central High School English composition teacher, **Bessie Whitford**, who stared down a roomful of young smartasses and told us that before she was done with us, we would be writers. I hope the others were as inspired as I've been.

The gifted screenwriter and novelist, **Walter Lockwood**, in whose Grand Rapids Community College creative writing class I learned to write believable dialogue. The short story, "Catch the High Tide," the facts of which are true, was written in his class.

The beloved people's chronicler on the *Grand Rapids Press*, **Tom Rademacher**, who has mentored me and praised my work.

My friend and fellow Gilmore Car Museum enthusiast, **Larry Baum**, whose interest in community service and great literature has made the world around him a better place.

My longtime Festival buddy, **Eileen Schwarz-Duty**, herself a gifted wordsmith, who read and purged the manuscript before my errors became the talk of the town.

The professionals, **Rolly Smith** of Gilson Graphics, and **Anne Huizenga** of Graphic Concepts, who turned this pile of paper into a real book.

And my many colleagues, near and far, whose integrity and dedication to our craft made what we did for a living far more than just voices in the wind. Also the countless authentic writers who shared with me their passion for writing and some of their secrets during our conversations on the Buck Matthews Show.

About the Author

 Although Buck Matthews has spent more than sixty years in radio and television, he has often thought of himself as a writer who just happened to earn a living in broadcasting. An arts and community service activist, he was awarded the Key to the City by two Grand Rapids mayors and received the Grand Rapids Arts Council's Festival award in 1982. His "Buck Matthews Show" on WOOD-TV, Grand Rapids, aired nearly 2,000 times over a nine-year period and was named the best of its kind in the nation in 1972 by the National Association of Television Program Executives.

His writing credits include numerous magazine, newspaper, and broadcast commentaries. *Getting Here* is his third book. His mystery novel, *Uncommon Women*, is available as an e-book on Amazon Kindle. *Soil, Soul, and Simplicity*, the light-hearted history of Marne United Methodist Church and the village of Marne, Michigan, is available at the church.

A Maryland native and U. S. Air Force veteran, Buck grew up in Washington, DC, and attended Ohio Wesleyan and Columbia Universities. He and his wife, Thelma, live in Jenison, Michigan. Their son and daughter and one grandson also live in the Grand Rapids area.

He's still writing.